FREE HELP FROM UNCLE SAM TO START YOUR OWN BUSINESS

(OR EXPAND THE ONE YOU HAVE)

REVISED EDITION

William Alarid
Gustav Berle

Puma Publishing Co.
Santa Maria, California

First Printing May 1988
Second Printing August 1988
Third Printing November 1988
Fourth Printing July 1989 Completely Revised
Fifth Printing October 1989

Library of Congress Cataloging-in-Publication Data

Alarid, William, 1936-
    Free help from Uncle Sam to start your own business (or expand
the one you have) / William Alarid, Gustav Berle. -- Rev. ed.
    208 p.   cm.
    Bibliography: p.
    Includes index.
    ISBN 0-940673-41-X (alk. paper)
    1. Small business--Government policy--United States--Handbooks,
manuals, etc. I. Berle, Gustav, 1920-   . II. Title.
    HD2346.U5A63   1989
    338.6'42'0973--dc19   89-31024
    CIP

Table of Contents

Chapter 5: ABOUT SHIPPING   65

Chapter 6: EVERYTHING YOU EVER WANTED TO KNOW, BUT WERE ASHAMED TO ASK (OR QUESTIONS THAT WOULD MAKE DR. RUTH BLUSH)   69

Chapter 7: FINANCIAL HELP 85

INTRODUCTION

Billions of dollars worth of loans and advice are being given away annually by Uncle Sam. No wonder he is often referred to as 'Uncle Sugar'! Are **you** getting your just share?

Free Help From Uncle Sam has attempted to seek out the places, the projects, and the paper mountains where such information is hidden. Not that Uncle Sam wants to hide these treasures from its citizens. It's just that there is so much of it.

Dozens of bureaus and hundreds of programs, some of them overlapping, make it difficult to find the one or ones that apply and appeal to you. Sometimes the language of bureaucratese obfuscates and confuses access to these programs. And yet, ironically enough, Congress has mandated these programs. The various departments **want** to give away their fiscal allotments or dispense their programs and information. If they don't, they might cease to exist. If they do not spend the money that is allocated to them this year, it will be withdrawn the next.

By the very size, by the very nature of the gigantic U.S. government, it is still difficult to find your way through the maze of a well-meaning bureaucracy.

While Big Business gets well-publicized support that goes into the hundreds of millions (such as savings and loan associations, Chrysler Corporation, et al.), it is the hundreds of thousands of small businesses that get much unpublicized support. Just look at the figures.

Ninety-seven percent of all U.S. businesses are classified as "small business" — that is, enterprises with gross volumes under $5,000,000 a year. It is to these that this book is directed and dedicated.

Among small businesses, two noticeable trends stand out:

(1) more and more minorities are entering the marketplace of entrepreneurs. Blacks and Orientals are in

the forefront. In fact, if you are a minority or of Hispanic origin, you will have a few points in your favor, and many of the programs listed in this volume point this out.

(2) more and more women, proportionately, are entering the world of independent entrepreneurs — foregoing the security of home and corporate life for the risky turbulence of independence. According to one national business counseling organization, SCORE, about 47% of all persons requesting counseling or attending going-into-business workshops are women.

Last year over 230,000 new small businesses were formed and nearly three times as many incorporations were listed. All of these entrepreneurs, whether just thinking about business, ready to enter it, or planning to expand an existing one, would be well advised to peruse the pages of this book. Somewhere in these pages is a program that can be of help — that can be a shortcut to information, success and profits.

Some of these programs and information are highly valuable regardless of price. You could not duplicate much of this information, because most of us do not have the resources. And the best thing is that you need to invest only a 25-cent postage stamp or use one single finger — the one you use to dial the appropriate department, and to say, "I read in *Free Help From Uncle Sam* that . . . ."

And if all else fails, if you absolutely cannot find the information you seek in this book, you can always pick up the phone, from anywhere in the U. S. A., and dial the U.S. Small Business Administration's toll-free hot line for the small business information you need. (800) 368-5855 is the number that unlocks a million dollars' worth of information.

W.A./G.B.

Chapter 1

HOW GOVERNMENT AID HAS BEEN USED BY OTHERS

Here are a few examples of how others have used government aid. We hope it gives you some ideas of new ways they can help you. If so, please let us know.

Teddy Roosevelt said, "I am as strong as a bull moose and you can work me all you want." As a taxpayer, you have a considerable investment in these resources. Use them.

We thank the many government agencies that sent us material for this and the following sections. We selected the following samples for you.

1. HOT DOG! MAINE'S SMALL BUSINESS PERSON OF THE YEAR (1987)

H. Allen Ryan worked for a hot dog and lunchmeat producer in the state of Maine. With the SBA's help he transformed it into a dynamo offering 4,000 different food and non-food items to 1,400 restaurants, schools, and hospitals.

"The local bank insisted on an SBA guarantee as part of their commitment, meaning that without SBA's help the whole deal was likely to die," disclosed Ryan.

"I found SBA to be detailed, professional, and very helpful during the negotiations for the guarantee. They asked tough questions as they sought to balance the interests of the taxpayer and their responsibility to assist small companies. In the end, they saved our deal."

"Without SBA's help I might not own our growing business today."

2. THE FASTEST GROWING HISPANIC FIRM IN ARIZONA

And the tenth fastest in the nation is Roberto Ruiz's Maya Construction. With the SBA's help sales went from $1,700 a year in 1978 to $23 million in 1987.

Ruiz has built everything from schools at Fort Huachuca to a water distribution system (including drinking fountains) for the National Park Service in the Grand Canyon. Maya has had private and state building, roadway, and underground water and sewer projects, as well.

Seeing himself "as a coach, not a captain" of his company, Ruiz likes to act "as a cheering section for employees, to tell them when they're on target and guide them when they're not." Twice a year, he retreats with his top managers for two days to plot Maya's business future.

Ruiz has garnered many accolades: Arizona Small Business Person of the Year (1983): National Minority Contractor of the Year, Department of Commerce (1984), and Department of the Interior (1986). SBA likes to think of itself as a cheering section for this intrepid Mexican-American.

3. FEDERAL EXPRESS: SBA WAS THERE AT THE CREATION

Federal Express vice president Fred Smith, whose family founded Dixie Greyhound, started his air package delivery service in May 1973 in Memphis, Tennessee. Undercapitalized and overreaching, the company had lost close to $7 million by summer. There was no partial bailout possible—Smith determined he needed no less than $24.5 million of investment capital (to be matched by banks) in order to service the dozens of cities that would make the new delivery concept both profitable and efficient. Meanwhile, as one report put it, "the company was being held together with bailing wire."

SBA's Small Business Investment Companies (SBICs) supplied 20 percent—or roughly $5 million—of financing needed by Federal Express in 1973 when the young firm was in its critical start-up years.

Some 51,000 people are working at Federal Express (up from only 518 at the time of SBA's involvement). The $3 billion company created a new concept in hard copy delivery and a whole industry of competitors as well.

4. FROM A $75 PARKING LOT STRIPER MACHINE TO RICHES

Steven Neighbors of Boise, Idaho swept parking lots as a schoolboy. He noticed that many lots needed fresh stripes to guide drivers into parking spaces. When the opportunity to purchase a $75 striping machine came along, he took it.

"I had a dream to start a road-striping business and was not taken seriously by anyone but the SBA. Their personnel listened seriously to a kid who looked fifteen, and set in motion for him to be trained to consider market, project goals, cash flow, etc. In essence, the Small Business Administration, with the commitment of a direct loan of

$10,000 and an investment of time, created a small businessman."

That time investment was provided chiefly by SBA's SCORE counselor Jim Cheatham, a retired engineer, and Nancy Guiles, a loan officer, in the Boise district office. The result is business history. Neighbors' company, Eterna-Line Corp., has been listed among *Inc.* magazine's 500 fastest-growing private companies in each of the past three years. Annual sales went from $5,000 at the time of the SBA loan to $10 million today. Currently there are 200 employees.

5. CANVAS TARPS MADE IN A BASEMENT

He invented a beltless tarp that rolls automatically over a truck full of grain. His hardwood veneers adorn many a renovated home across the land. But what makes Ed Shorma most happy is that there are at least fifteen nationalities among his 220 employees at Wahpeton Canvas in North Dakota.

You wouldn't expect Malaysians and Indonesians to work in 30-below-zero weather, or what Northerners call "white-out" storms. But Shorma has sponsored dozens of refugees from many lands, and has gone one step further: he has given them jobs.

Up-from-the-bootstraps stories don't involve SBA — that's the conventional misconception. In 1970, after an unsuccessful stint at farming and a term in the state legislature, Shorma wanted to go full tilt with canvas-making. To effect a move from a basement to a downtown space, SBA loaned Shorma $75,000. The extra space was put to immediate use manufacturing original equipment seats for Canadian farm equipment makers — helping the trade balance in the days when it wasn't so unbalanced.

At the time of SBA's first loan, Wahpeton Canvas had gross annual sales of $147,000, and seventeen employees. Today the company sells $12 million worth of goods a year, and has 220 employees. Not a bad return on investment!

6. THE PICKLE KING

Like relish on your hot dog? Have a yen for sweet (or dill) pickles? Chances are sometime in the past thirty years, most Americans have enjoyed a product of Atkins Pickle Company of Atkins, Arkansas. Think of the Ozarks the next time you taste a good, long, green pickle. And think of SBA—without it Atkins would have been a modest pickle packer indeed.

In 1959 the pickle company received a $350,000 SBA loan when it had less than $1 million in annual sales and 100 employees. Today Atkins Pickle has $20 million in yearly sales and 400 employees.

7. FIRED MAN BUILDS UNIFORM CHAIN

"I was fired into greatness," jokes Harvey Hafetz of his dismissal from a job as a sales representative for a cosmetics distributor in 1971. Of course, that's today—*then* it was a painful experience.

Harvey's wife, Zena, had decided just that year to leave her job as an elementary school teacher and try another challenge. The couple purchased a small uniform shop in Reading, Pennsylvania, as an investment and to give Zena part-time on-the-job training for a new career. But when Harvey lost his job, he joined his wife at the little store. Z & H Uniforms was born.

Today, the company has twenty retail stores, mostly in shopping malls and eleven leased departments catering primarily to health care professionals. A contract sales department furnishes executive-type apparel, hospitality, food service, and industrial-type clothing to industry.

In 1985 Z & H added ten stores after acquiring a Philadelphia-based competitor's stores with the help of a $600,000 SBA-guaranteed loan from Meridian Bank. The firm had 75 employees then: only three years later, it has 170. Annual sales volume has doubled in that time, from $3.5 million to $7 million.

8. FISHING BOAT SUCCESS

Ever heard of a start-up fishing boat? It happens.

In 1986 with a loan of $500,000, SBA helped launch the Huntress II and its captain, Richard Goodwin, into the fishing waters off the coast of Rhode Island. According to James Hague, district director in the Providence office, "Our major consideration in approving the SBA portion of this loan was that under-utilized species such as mackerel, hake, herring, and scup, not widely consumed in the United States, would be processed and exported to foreign markets such as Japan, Spain, and other European countries."

The Huntress II fishing operations employ forty, and annual sales in the first year were $2.4 million, substantially exceeding expectations. In the first half of 1987, sales already matched the figures of the entire previous year. Huntress, Inc., recently purchased a second ship for $1.2 million which will employ up to fifteen new workers.

"The fishing industry in Rhode Island has always been a risky business," said Buddy Violet of Ocean State Business Development Authority (OSBDA). "But these new boats are to fishing what Babe Ruth was to baseball. Phenomenal!" Violet noted that SBA was a crucial partner in the novel project. The State of Rhode Island "could not have gone anywhere else to cinch the deal but SBA," he said.

9. GOV'T AT APPLE'S CORE

In 1977 an SBA-backed Small Business Investment Company (SBIC) provided $504,000 in equity financing to Steven Jobs and Stephen Wozniak, founders of Apple Computer. The company made $42,000 in profit that year. Only ten years later, Apple Computing has annual sales of $2.6 billion and employs 6,500 people.

10. MEXICAN RESTAURANT BIG HIT

Who said SBA won't back a start-up restaurant?

In 1970, Mariano Martinez, Jr. gathered every resource he could to start a restaurant in Dallas' Old Town Shopping Center. He had $5,000 of his own money, and he borrowed $5,000 from his father, $5,000 from a friend, and $51,000 from SBA. By year's end, Martinez had 60 employees and annual sales of $350,000.

Over the next twelve years, Martinez opened a second restaurant in Arlington, Texas, with SBA help ($390,000 loan), and another in Dallas with a $243,000 loan.

Today, employment at the firm has increased to 200, and annual sales exceed $3 million. The original loan is paid, while the others remain current.

11. HOW ABOUT A JOINT?

Osteoarthritis, a degenerative joint disease, affects millions, sometimes requiring an implant. The SBA has participated in many of 300,000 total joint procedures in operating rooms in 1986. Here's how.

Orthopedic implants are traditionally manufactured by giant pharmaceutical corporations. But in 1978, SBA took a chance on a small company in Warsaw, Indiana, called Biomet, whose first-year sales were only $17,000. It guaranteed a $500,000 loan to the owners, Dr. Dane Miller, Niles Noblitt, Jerry Ferguson, and Ray Harroff.

With only its four owners as employees then, Biomet today has 530 workers, and annual sales of over $55 million. The company's phenomenal success—due to technical innovations and rapid delivery of its implants—has made it the 16th fastest growing NASDAQ (National Association of Security Dealers' Automated Quotation System) company in 1987, and the fifth largest manufacturer or orthopedic implant devices in the world.

12. PLENTY OF BREAD IN THE U.S.

Samir Saleh had to flee Lebanon in 1976 when civil war broke out. He came to the U.S. and with his uncle's help started a bakery.

Uncle Moussa also "was aware of the resources of SBA," according to Samir. At first there was a pessimistic assessment by SCORE counselor and internationally known baking consultant Frank Dadon. But soon Fred Fried, a retired Westinghouse financial supervisor and SCORE counselor, was giving the Salehs help with business planning and accounting. Along the way two SBA loans gave the Salehs a boost. In 1983, a $100,000 loan covered new machinery and a small debt to a credit union. In 1986, a loan of $178,000 helped the bakery expand to four times its original size.

"For people in our situation, SBA's assistance is the best thing that ever existed," said a grateful Samir, who cannot see returning to war-torn Lebanon: "The way it looks, we're here to stay. Raleigh is my hometown." As Joe puts it, "only in America could three young immigrant boys with little previous business experience come so far in ten short years."

13. SCORE CLASSES IN AN INDIANA PRISON

"Afraid? You bet we were."

Richard Dasse of the Northwest Indiana Chapter of the Service Corps of Retired Executives (SCORE) recalls when he and his SCORE associate began providing management training seminars in a most unusual place — an Indiana prison. "We feared for our safety, and we really wondered if anyone would have the intellectual capacity or be interested."

Now, after three years of providing assistance at the Westville Correctional Center, Dasse acknowledges, "This is not exactly a Sunday School atmosphere," but adds:

"We're tremendously impressed. The interest is great, and we've actually encountered some brilliant individuals."

The courses offered at Westville, a medium-security institution located about an hour's drive from Chicago, are similar to those a small business person might find "on the outside" — a pre-business workshop, one on small business management, another on problems peculiar to small business, and another on small business sales.

14. INTEL — A GIANT IN BYTE-SIZE CHIPS

It is the eighth largest manufacturer of semiconductors in the world (and one of only three American companies in the top ten). It is responsible for two of the major post-war innovations in microelectronics that have made today's electronic age possible — large scale integrated (LSI) memory and the microprocessor. Its computer chips, software, and minicomputers drive everything from digital gasoline pumps to scanner cash registers in supermarkets.

It is Intel. And when it was a one-year-old baby company in 1969 — with 218 employees and $565,874 in sales — it received SBA-backed Small Business Investment Company equity of $299,390. Today Intel has 19,200 employees and annual sales of $1.9 billion. It has often approached and even surpassed achievements of Motorola and Texas Instruments — two corporate giants when Intel was a start-up small business.

In 1987, 39 percent of Intel's total revenues came from abroad, making the company one of the top fifty U.S.-based manufacturing exporters. Who ever thought that a well-placed bit of SBA-backed equity twenty years ago would be a key force in helping to right our trade deficit?

15. HARDWARE STORE IN WYOMING

The number one hardware store in the 1,500-store coast-to-coast chain rests in the mountain town of Casper,

Wyoming. Says owner Ed Bratt, "If it hadn't been for the SBA loan, I doubt we would have even got off the ground."

In 1974, when Ed and Joyce Bratt tried to find funds to start a retail hardware store, they were shut out by banks. But by year's end SBA came to the rescue with a start-up guaranteed loan of $175,000. "On opening day we sold twelve percent of our inventory," Ed relates. No surprise that the loan was paid off in three years. With ten employees then, the Bratts now employ 39; their annual sales are $3 million.

16. ICE CREAM SUCCESS DESPITE TROUBLES

Life with the 140-year-old Applegate Farm in Montclair, New Jersey was anything but bright for Betty Vhay. Since purchasing the dairy farm in 1981 with her husband, Vhay has endured more than the usual set of hard knocks. Money was chronically low; neighbors brought a lawsuit against the farm over "loud" machinery that was making ice cream (and making the place a "hang-out" for area teenagers); she went through a bitter divorce. It seemed to her at times that the circumstances of the farm's purchase were an ill omen: after losing an unborn child in a car accident, she had taken $100,000 in settlement money to stake her future on Applegate Farm.

With two children to support by herself, Vhay pulled out all stops in the search for money to help the ice cream operation. Bank after bank turned her down as a credit risk.

Then in January 1987, the Money Store Investment Corporation took a chance on Vhay and provided her with an SBA-guaranteed loan of $170,000. For the first time since 1981, she had working capital, was sole owner, and recorded her first profit.

In 1981, Vhay employed 10; today she employs 52, most of whom are teenagers outfitted with their first job as ice cream barflies. Annual sales in 1987 were $700,000, a sizable increase over the $420,000 figure in 1981.

17. MEL FARR SCORES TOUCHDOWN IN CARS

For every sports star who makes it big, there are many others who lose out when the limelight fades. Bad management skills, drugs, naive investments — these are only a few of the pitfalls. But Mel Farr, former All-American halfback for UCLA and star runner for the Detroit Lions, stutter-stepped away from those things.

Mel Farr Ford, Inc., in Oak Park, Michigan, is one of the largest car dealers in America, ranked 37th of the nation's top 100 U. S. black-owned businesses by *Black Enterprise*. But Farr does not forget a helping hand.

"When SBA granted my loan it was the very key to what I needed at that time," Farr recalls. "Without it, I more than likely would have had to postpone or even forget about my dream of becoming an automobile dealer."

Retail car sales were bleak in the late seventies. Mel Farr Ford, Inc. was born at that time (1978) and in two years the company had sustained severe losses and employees were halved in number, to 45.

But in 1980, SBA made an auto dealer loan of $200,000 to Farr, when sales were $6 million. Today there are two more Mel Farr dealerships (Lincoln-Mercury) in Detroit and Aurora, Colorado, and aggregate sales are $52 million. There are 140 employees.

Farr out!

18. BLACK EX-MARINE AND JEWISH FEMALE CONSULTANT CREATE UNITED NATIONS DRILLING COMPANY

A black man and a Jewish woman — not your usual business team in critical pre-construction testing! It happened in the Bronx.

In a highly specialized field hardly open to minorities and women, Garrett W. Brown, a Vietnam veteran, and Honie Ann Peacock, a consultant in employee relations, drill for "dirt" samples in the chasms of the Big Apple as Python Drilling and Testing.

1980 — their first year — was not a good one for construction. There were nights without dinner and weeks when payroll was met on a credit card. Peacock, a single parent, took two outside jobs and worked full time without pay to help get the fledgling company off the ground. Brown, an ex-Marine sergeant who specialized in heavy construction equipment and diesel engines, brought 20 years of experience in the construction industry to the company. He designed and built their first drill rig in his living room.

Peacock wrote the loan proposal and marketing plan that enabled the company to receive a $50,000 direct loan from SBA which bought them their first big drill rig and truck. Today their 16-person crew has been trained completely from within and represents a virtual "United Nations," including Blacks, Filipinos, Hispanics, Irish, and Finns, both male and female.

Though it has been an uphill struggle to gain the confidence of their numerous clients, Brown and Peacock maintain a positive attitude. And why not? From the time of SBA's loan, annual sales have grown from $30,000 to over $1 million.

19. DOUGHNUT-MAKING MACHINE EXPORT SUCCESS

Lil' Orbits, a Minneapolis manufacturer of a miniature doughnut-making machine and doughnut mix, turned to the Department of Commerce for export assistance. The Department provided publicity with their New Product Information Service (NPIS) along with a description in *Commercial News* magazine, both distributed widely abroad. The products were also exhibited at a Fast Food Exhibition in Paris, France in March of 1988.

"It looks like we're in the export business to stay," reports Lil' Orbits president Ed Anderson. "Results to date are gratifying. Worldwide publicity through this program has resulted in sales of the machine to firms in Japan, Thailand, West Germany, and the West Indies.

These efforts resulted in $575,000 in sales. Inquiries from Jamaica, the Philippines, Singapore, Norway, Korea, and Denmark are expected to yield further sales.

20. THERMAL BAGS BY INGRID

A 12-employee, Des Plaines, Illinois firm makes insulated bags for catering and food delivery. In five yeares the firm has gone from zero to approximately $900,000 in sales.

Ingrid exhibited at a trade show attended by foreign firms but their orders were too large for her to fulfill.

She contacted the Commerce Department's International Trade Administration and described her problem. They had her attend an export financing seminar.

"Now we know how to do it," Ingrid says. "We couldn't have done it without the guidance we received from the Commerce Department."

They now export to England, Norway, Australia, Sweden, the Netherlands, Spain, France, Mexico and Panama.

21. REBUILT TRANSMISSIONS AND ENGINES

Tracom, Inc., a small Fort Worth company, rebuilds automotive transmissions and engines. The Department of Commerce consulted with them about the potential for exporting, identified the appropriate foreign firms and helped prepare a sales letter.

Among other sales was one to an Australian distributor for $470,000!

Sales increased from $250,000 a year to $2.5 million in 1987. Currently they sell to many foreign markets including the United Kingdom, Kuwait, and New Zealand.

22. WHOLESALE COMPUTER SUPPLIES

Digital Storage International, a company with six employees, handles magnetic media such as diskettes, tapes and data cartridges in Columbus, Ohio. A slow domestic market compelled them to look elsewhere. The Department of Commerce's Agent Distributor Service (ADS) helped locate oversea representatives. The Cincinnati DOC office also provided export counseling. This help led to expansion into 28 countries.

23. DEPARTMENT OF ENERGY HELPS SOFTWARE FIRM

The Department of Energy funds projects under its Small Business Innovation Research (SBIR) program. It helped Emerson and Stern Associates, a small San Diego firm, develop software for elementary and junior high students using Apple computers. They then negotiated a licensing agreement with a major software publisher for production and distribution.

24. DEPARTMENT OF HEALTH HELPS LAUNCH FIRM

Data Sciences had two employees and a good idea. They wanted to develop devices to help gather information for pharmaceutical firms from experiments via an implantable transmitter that monitors numerous body functions. They presented the idea to the Department of Health and Human Services, and received financial backing.

As a result of this help, Data Sciences has grown to 12 people and is selling about $20,000 worth of devices per month.

25. DEPARTMENT OF DEFENSE FUNDS RESEARCH

Ultramet, a Pacoima, California firm, had an idea for a coating for rocket engines that won't corrode and is tolerant of high temperatures. The DOD's Small Business Innovation Research program provided funds to develop it. Ultramet is now selling this product to major aerospace companies.

26. NATIONAL SCIENCE FOUNDATION HELPS COMPANY FIGHT POLLUTION

Tracer Technologies, located in Newton, Maine, wanted to build an anti-pollution device. Fund from National Science Foundation through its Small Business Innovation Research program allowed them to do that. They came up with a gadget that can separate chlorinated hydrocarbons so that they can be burned in ordinary furnaces. A service business was launched as a result.

27. PIZZA ANALYSIS

The owner of a pizza shop was having problems with pizza consistency, and productivity. The Commerce Productivity Center sent information on statistical process control, cause and effect diagramming, and other techniques so he could monitor and analyze the process of preparing pizza, and determine the probable causes of the consistency problem. He was also provided information on providing quality service to the customer, measuring productivity, how to study and improve workflow/equipment location.

Japanese housekeeping "Five S" principles were instigated:

1. sort out the clutter
2. set things in order and standardize
3. shine equipment, tools and workplace
4. share information, no searching
5. stick to the rules.

Other principals that were taught are:

— Clutter hides problems
— Everything should have an "address"
— Storage spaces should be self-regulating through visual controls
— Cleaning equipment is a form of inspection
— Make information easily accessible; for example, place operating procedures on machines.

28. CULTURAL HELP

The American manager of a small west coast electronics firm was having problems managing the engineers of Singapore and American Chinese descent. The Commerce Productivity Center sent information on the work-related values, attitudes and habits of these ethnic groups which are different than those of American workers.

29. THE EFFECT OF COLD ON WORKERS

A northeast construction contractor's job was delayed by legal problems. Outdoor construction was going to have to be done in winter instead of in warmer weather, as had been planned. The owner wanted to know how much productivity would decline because of cold, inclement weather so he could adjust his prices. The Commerce Productivity Center located and sent formulas and information on how construction productivity is affected at different temperatures.

30. THE EFFECT OF LIGHTING

A floor plan for remodeling some offices at a company had been developed. The plan called for every worker to have a window in their office or by his desk. The boss didn't think this was a good idea. The remodeling planners called to find out if employees with windows in their offices are more productive. The Commerce Productivity Center researched the problem and offered the findings. Workers with windows are happier, but not necessarily more productive. The real issue is proper lighting. Windows and sunlight aren't necessarily appropriate. The best lighting is that which is designed for the particular tasks being performed; proper lighting improves performance. And lighting can be designed for energy efficiency and save money.

31. THE EFFECT OF NIGHTSHIFT

A contractor was remodeling an office building's interior during the daytime. The remodeling made so much noise that the building's occupants couldn't get any work done. The occupants got a court injunction forcing the contractor to do the remodeling work at night.

When the nightwork started, the productivity of the contractor's workforce dropped dramatically. The contractor called for help, the Commerce Productivity Center researched the problem and found the probable cause.

People have an internal biological clock set by routine. Our bodies tell us when to wake up, when to eat, and when to go to sleep. When the workers suddenly shifted to night work, their biological clocks were disrupted. It produced a jet-lag-type effect.

Studies show that an individual's productivity can decline until the biological clock adjusts to the new routine. Also, there was a stress-producing disruption in the workers' personal routines and schedules.

32. SAVING MONEY ON WINE

A small winery was losing money and needed to cut its costs. The winery had also been hiring full-time employees for jobs that took less than full time. The Commerce Productivity Center provided information on how to study the production process to identify waste in areas such as transportation, work in process, machine setup, non-value adding activities, storage, defects, etc., and on developing multi-skilled, multi-functional workers.

33. HELP MAKE A GOOD IMPRESSION

The International Operations Group helps small businesses with their uncertainties concerning foreign clients. For example:

—The president of a small consulting company heard that a potential Japanese client was coming to town the next day, on extremely short notice, and would be available for meetings. The International Operations Group helped the company locate information about the company, its products, and recent company activities, so that the consultant made a favorable impression and acquired the Japanese firm as a client.

34. HELP ON A HOME-BASED CUT-FLOWER BUSINESS

A North Carolina woman wanted information on producing and marketing cut flowers and herbs in the mid-South. She contacted the Department of Agriculture's ATTRA service and received fact sheets, booklets on home-based businesses and referrals to experts.

ATTRA (Appropriate Technology Transfer for Rural Areas) specializes in low-input sustainable agriculture (USA). Other help they've given involved; raising earthworms, mushrooms, aquaculture, marketing herbs, establishing farmers markets, farm management computer software, raising fallow deer and elk, farm scale composting, direct marketing, biorational pest management, nitrogen release from green manure and organic certification, alternative farming techniques that minimize off-farm purchases of fertilizers and pesticides is also emphasized.

35. EVER BEEN BURIED BY YOUR WORK?

A rapid transit system contractor was involved in trenching and excavating and asked for help in protecting his workers. A Department of Labor consultant in OSHA was called for a confidential, risk-free evaluation (i.e., the consultant would not issue any citations for violations of state or federal safety standards). The consultant arrived the day after a heavy rain and found some workers in a twelve-foot deep trench that was not shored nor sloped. He advised immediate evacuation; the supervisor ordered all workers out of the trench. Ten minutes later the sides of the trench gave way. The workers would have been buried. The consultant showed the contractor a six-step plan to resume work safely.

36. THE GOVERNMENT CURES HEADACHES

A small auto parts custom electroplating shop with four employees had trouble with the workers having headaches. They had recently installed a gas-fired hot-water boiler. An OSHA consultant analyzed the problem: Carbon monoxide from the boiler was coming into the building because there was no vent to bring fresh air to the boiler, and the exhaust fans, instead of helping, were making the problem worse. The employer, with the consultant's help, was able to fix the problem easily.

37. MEAT PACKER GETS SOLUTION TO HAZARD PROBLEM

A meat packer had employees working on a slippery platform 10 feet above a concrete floor. The employees stood on the edge working with power tools on carcasses suspended from a moving conveyor.

The platform was slippery with animal fat. Guardrails could not be used since they would inhibit the conveyor. The employer contacted other meat packers and found that none of them had a solution.

An OSHA consultant gave a free, confidential, no-hassle safety survey. He recommended the employees wear a body belt with a lanyard attached by a sliding ring to an overhead rail. The employees thought they wouldn't like it, but after trying it found it convenient and comfortable, and it did not slow them up.

38. CENSUS DATA HELPS SALES

A manufacturer of corrugated boxes contacted the Census Bureau to help him analyze his sales in the state of Arizona. At the time he was selling primarily to food packaging companies. Using census data he found the market potential was 15 times larger than he was experiencing. Lumber, pottery, and glass industries in Arizona also needed his products and he successfully marketed to these previously unidentified customers.

A manufacturer of products for dairy farms used census data to locate counties with large numbers of dairy farms. By next determining which were the most prosperous, he was able to optimize his marketing efforts.

39. GOVERNMENT PUBLICATION BRINGS $2,500,000 IN SALES

Barrier Industries of Baton Rouge, Louisiana manufactures an insecticidal paint called "Bug-X." They approached the Department of Commerce, who suggested worldwide exposure in the U.S. Government publication *Commercial News USA*. Information on "Bug-X" appeared in the July 1985 issue and resulted in $2,500,000 in sales. The firm has signed six overseas agents and reports another eighteen under negotiation.

40. TEENAGE LANDSCAPE ENTREPRENEUR

A Pennsylvania teenager applied for and received a Department of Agriculture Youth Project Loan to start a landscaping business. He purchased all of the necessary equipment and operated the business for three years before moving on to bigger things.

41. GRANT FOR SOLAR-POWERED OUTHOUSE

A Missouri inventor applied for and received a grant to research and construct a solar-energized outhouse. The Above Ground Aerobic and Solar-Assisted Composting Toilet uses solar energy to decompose waste.

42. SCORE HELPS TWO YOUNG LADIES LAUNCH BUTCHER SHOP

An old-fashioned butcher shop in which you can buy ready-cut and portioned meats, but also obtain cut-to-order steaks and roasts, is the unusual business of a pair of young women from Ohio. The father of one has a meat market in another area and he taught his daughter the business. With the help of a knowledgeable SCORE counselor they were able to draft a credible business plan and obtain an SBA-guaranteed loan of $150,000. The money afforded the two entrepreneurs was used to purchase display cases, a walk-in freezer, smokehouse and double oven. With continued help from SCORE counselors, lots of enthusiasm and hard work, the two women recreated a business that had been a vanishing breed—and customers have been coming from near and far because they learned that the shop's products were truly a cut above.

43. SCORE HELPS PREVENT LOSS OF LIFETIME SAVINGS

This is a negative success story and it could apply to any business anywhere. This one comes from San Diego where a man who had been pensioned from a large company had a bundle of cash to invest. He liked the liquor business— quick turnover, constant business, easy-to-handle merchandise. A business broker offered him two stores on the market for $300,000. Fortunately, even though he had his mind pretty well made up to buy them, he followed a friend's advice and contacted the local SCORE office.

A counselor with long years of liquor store experience did his own investigation of the stores—checking inventory, merchandise, traffic flow, competition, service handling, pricing—and then recommended against the acquisition. It was $100,000 overpriced. The locations were weak. The competition from big chains and discount stores was overwhelming. Despite his enthusiasm, the would-be entrepreneur finally realized the SCORE counselor's wisdom and withdrew his offer — possibly saving his lifetime assets before, like alcohol, they could evaporate.

44. SCORE DOUBLES JEWELRY DESIGNER'S BUSINESS

A jewelry designer in Seattle happened to see a story on SCORE in the papers. It stimulated her to seek free counseling and explore her desire to go into a retail business. The counselor guided her first of all in executing a viable business plan, then advised her on seeking and securing a good location.

A seven step plan was developed under which she doubled her business after the first year. The counselor still helps after four years, including proposing a "Men's Night" promotion before Christmas, which turned out to be the year's most productive sales event.

45. RAGS TO RICHES FOR FASHION DESIGNER

The mother of two children, divorced, and struggling along on sheer guts and hard work, the young black designer in Massachusetts heard about SCORE and requested an appointment. Fortunately, the assigned counselor evaluated her talent and enthusiasm accurately.

Her unique use of knit fabrics and design, plus the fact that she is an attractive young black woman, combined to make her a "media event." They planned an extensive publicity campaign that attracted a number of local notables and generated considerable press coverage.

A well-executed projection and business plan enabled her to get an SBA-guaranteed loan that allowed for the addition of several sewing machines and more workers. Currently she heads her own design studio, producing fashions

under her own label. The line is scheduled to go national. She was selected as "Woman of the Year" in New England.

46. LONG-TERM RELATIONSHIPS WITH SCORE

Supermarkets are admittedly one of the toughest businesses next to running a restaurant. This Indiana family supermarket has had the longest counseling arrangement of any business in the U.S. — and all with the local SCORE counselors. For sixteen years they have been advised by one or several members of the Service Corps of Retired Executives.

Ownership is now in its second generation. Ironically, the family-owned business was encouraged to take over the vacant premises of a former Kroger supermarket that had a good and established location.

SCORE counseled budgeting, financial planning, quality assurance, promotion and the kind of public relations that chain stores could not provide. They helped the family to get into computerization as well as guide them into each step of planned expansions.

47. DAY CARE CENTER JUST KID'S STUFF TO SCORE

Reading in the papers that day care centers are one of the most needed and hottest enterprises, a man-and-wife team of corporate executives saw an opportunity to go into business for themselves. They decided to start an upscale after-school youth-sitting service for latchkey kids in their Connecticut community.

The local SCORE counselors helped them set up a proper business plan and, to conserve limited capital, suggested a direct mail campaign to specific, better neighborhoods. Another counselor suggested publicity for the unique venture that was quite successful.

They opened "Kidstop" with seven young customers. Within the year the business had expanded to 64. "The SCORE counselors were a dramatic help to us," said the owners. "We hope to continue using their expertise."

48. ORNAMENTAL PLANT BUSINESS BLOOMS OVERSEAS

A large grower of **ornamental plants** in Florida was trying to sell his plants overseas where a potentially uncrowded and lucrative market awaited him. However, he found that it took more plants to fill a traditional container than he could produce, and more expertise and money than he could manage. So he explored the idea with other growers throughout the state. The result was a cooperative association of growers.

They hired a coordinator-promoter familiar with marketing in Holland and Western Europe. In 1985, the first year of the joint effort, the cooperative group sold $2 million worth.

The best was yet to come, however. A SCORE counselor helped reorganize the co-op and initiate a newsletter and promotion material to use at European trade fairs. In 1986 export volume increased six times to $12 million. It currently is $18 million and growing.

49. INVENTOR GETS HELP FROM THE DEPARTMENT OF ENERGY

A Detroit, Michigan inventor developed a system that senses knocking in an automobile engine and controls the spark timing in individual cylinders. The idea was submitted to the Office of Energy-Related Inventions run by the National Institute of Standards and Technology (formerly National Bureau of Standards).

The invention got a favorable review and the government assisted him in bringing it to market. The inventor licensed his system to Ford Motor Co. in exchange for royalties.

Chapter 2

ASSISTANCE
AND INFORMATION

STARTERS

Where to Go First

Where do you start if (1) you currently are not in business and (2) would like to learn how to avoid common pitfalls and (3) want to take advantage of the experience of others?

The following four organizations will help point you in the right direction:

1. The Business Assistance Program, formerly known as **The Roadmap Program**, guides business to appropriate contacts. It is run by the Business Liaison Office of the Department of Commerce. They can answer such questions as:

What sources can help me start a business?

How can I sell my products or services to the Federal Government?

Where do I find overseas buyers?

Where can I get federal business loans?

Where can I get information on what the government is buying?

Where can I find the manufacturer of a particular product?

What associations serve my industry?

Where can I get information on patents, trademarks, and copyrights?

How can I market my invention?

Where can I get information on exporting and importing?

Who can advise me on unfair trade practices?

Where can I get debt collection guidelines?

Where can I get federal statistics?

Where can I get company lists?

How do I register my company name?

The office develops and promotes a cooperative working relationship and ensures effective communication between the Department of Commerce and the business community. It provides assistance to businesses which desire help in dealing with the Federal Government.

Professional staff members provide guidance through the Federal maze: answer inquiries concerning Government policies, programs, and services, and provide information on published materials on a variety of topics. It also serves as a focal point for Department of Commerce agencies' contact with the business community. Write or call: Gordon Schmidt or Martha Finerty, Business Liaison Office, Department of Commerce, Room 5898C, 14th & Constitution Avenue, N.W., Washington, DC 20230. Contact (202) 377-3176.

2. Federal Information Centers can also help you find the right answer. Often they will have copies of commonly used forms, such as copyright forms, that they will send from a telephoned request. These centers are a focal point for information about the Federal Government.

Centers assist people who have questions about Federal services, programs, and regulations, but do not know where to turn for an answer. FIC information specialists either answer an inquirer's questions directly, or perform the necessary research to locate and refer the inquirer to the expert best able to help.

There are currently 21 cities with an FIC and an additional 51 cities are connected to the nearest center by telephone tieline. Statewide toll-free '800' service is available to the residents of four states: Iowa, Kansas, Missouri, and Nebraska.

3. The toll-free Small Business Answer Desk handles about 84,000 inquiries per year, and is expected to double with the installation of an automatic answering system in 1989. Ask them for their "Small Business Startup Kit."

Run by the Small Business Administration, the Answer Desk is a nationwide, toll-free (800) telephone service to help small business persons needing help or guidance with problems connected with their firm or to deal with the complexities of government. It is an information and referral service guiding callers to the correct source for a definitive answer to inquiries relating to government regulations, government, and private source business assistance.

In most cases, the information or referral requested can be handled immediately by the Answer Desk staff, supported by rotators from all of the SBA's program areas and a variety of resource materials.

The Answer Desk focuses on Federal Government programs and regulations, but also provides information about state, municipal, and private sector agencies. It does not provide legal, accounting, or managerial advice. They refer such inquiries to appropriate sources, such as lawyers, accountants, SBA field offices, and appropriate government agencies.

The Answer Desk enables the SBA to become aware of the problems and issues of the small business community, which ultimately helps goverment do a better job of helping small business. Call toll free (800) 368-5855 or, if in the Washington area, (202) 653-7561.

4. New Business Incubation Centers Referral Service. Information is provided about the location of specific incubation centers which could help a smaller business.

Incubation centers are special facilities which offer a new business the facilities and business assistance which could make the difference in a firm's success. Since most of these centers are new, this office is maintaining a special file of the services and specialization of each center.

Call (202) 653-7880 and ask for Tom Lorentzen or John Shrewder, or write Private Sector Initiatives Office, Small Business Administration, 1441 L Street NW, Room 317, Washington, DC 20416.

THE BEST PROBLEM SOLVERS

Once you've gathered some basic information or start running into problems, try these fixer-uppers:

Services Corps of Retired Executives (SCORE) assists with free business counseling and training. They can get you out of the red faster than Rambo. SCORE exists solely for the benefit of the small business community. For anyone who is in — or is considering entering into — a small business, SCORE offers many services that might well be of critical importance to his or her success. SCORE makes no charge for counseling services, but usually charges a nominal amount for participating in training and workshop sessions.

Small business clients should be encouraged to take advantage of any of the following SCORE services that may meet their needs.

(1) **Counseling:** Both those who are considering entering a business enterprise and those who are already in a small business may benefit from the experience of successful, retired executives who are familiar with similar businesses. The advice furnished by SCORE counselors may be directed towards solving a particular problem or toward planning for future growth.

(2) **Training:** Broadly focused pre-startup business workshops are offered periodically, as well as more specialized classes, seminars, and conferences concerning topics of great value to certain segments of the business community. Subjects such as business organization, site selection, trade promotion, marketing, accounting, taxation, and financing are a few examples of the specialized training available.

(3) **Information:** Advice on obtaining and utilizing the professional services of lawyers, accountants, bankers, advertising agencies, and others, as well as the resources of government agencies, is provided upon request.

The primary purpose of SCORE is to render a community service by providing, without charge, the expert assistance of its volunteer counselors in solving the problems encountered by small businesses. In addition to a substantial number of retired executives and managers, the membership of SCORE chapters throughout the country includes many individuals who have not yet retired from active employment and are enrolled in its ACE (Active

Corps of Executives) component. Volunteer counselors who are qualified to furnish specialized counseling and training based upon their extensive and widely varied business and professional experience are selected.

To locate a SCORE chapter near you, look in the blue section of the phone book for the nearest SBA office or call (202) 653-6279. (Try the Small Business Answer Desk first.) Written inquiries should be addressed to: National SCORE Office, Small Business Administration, 655 15th St. NW, Suite 901, Washington, DC 20005-5742.

Chapter 3

NEW PRODUCTS

Each year government laboratories invent hundreds of new items which can be licensed by you, often on an exclusive basis. For example, 27% of NASA's patents are turned over to private industry via these agreements. Currently there are over 7,000 patents that are available for license.

1. LICENSE A GOVERNMENT INVENTION

A weekly newsletter, *Government Inventions for Licensing*, presents summaries (abstracts) of new inventions. All inventions are available for licensing (often exclusive). The newsletter describes some 1,200 new inventions each year. Annually, all inventions are presented in the *Catalog of Government Inventions Available for Licensing*. This catalog arranges descriptions of these 1,200 inventions under 41 subject areas for easy reference.

There is also a service named *Tech Notes*. *Tech Notes* provide illustrated monthly fact sheets of new processes and products developed by Federal agencies and their contractors. Each fact sheet details a specific invention, process, software, material, instrument or technique selected for its potential for commercial development or practical application.

Annual collections of all *Tech Notes* are available as the *Federal Technical Catalog*.

For more information contact: National Technical Information Service (NTIS), Center for the Utilization of Federal Technology (CUFT), Department of Commerce, 5285 Port Royal Road, Springfield, VA 22161. Phone (703) 487-4732.

2. GETTING YOUR INVENTION EVALUATED (AND PERHAPS SOME CASH TOO).

If your invention is energy related, you can get a free evaluation of its commercial feasibility and perhaps a grant to develop it further.

The **Energy Related Inventions Office** encourages innovation in non-nuclear energy technology by helping individual inventors and small R&D companies develop promising energy-related inventions. It evaluates all submitted inventions and recommends those that are promising to the Department of Energy (DOE).

The evaluation criteria are: technical feasibility, degree of energy impact, commercial potential, and intrinsic technical merit. DOE then reviews the recommended inventions and, working closely with the inventor, determines the next reasonable step for the invention and how much money it will take. Most often, support takes the form of a one-time-only cash grant and technical assistance in developing linkages with the private sector.

Contact: Energy Related Inventions Office, National Institute of Standards and Technology (formerly National Bureau of Standards), Department of Commerce, Building 202, Room 209, Gaithersburg, MD 20899. Phone (301) 975-5500.

3. PUT GOVERNMENT EXPERTS
TO WORK FOR YOU

The **Applied Technology Office** works with hundreds of Federal laboratories and agencies to make selected technologies, facilities, and expertise available to U.S. businesses. Acting as a special information resource for all agencies, the office offers special information announcing selected Federal technology and resources.

Ask for a copy of brochure PR801 and the *Directory of Federal Laboratory and Technology Resources*, which provides direct access to hundreds of Federal laboratories wishing to work with U.S. businesses.

Contact: Applied Technology Office, National Technical Information Service (NTIS), Center for the Utilization of Federal Technology (CUFT), Department of Commerce, 5285 Port Royal Road, Springfield, VA 22161. Phone (703) 487-4650.

4. AUTOMATIC AWARENESS OF WHAT'S
BEING PATENTED CONCERNING
YOUR SPECIALTY

If you have a particular interest, it's a good idea to keep abreast of what others are doing. Often after receiving a patent you may wish to contact the inventors or you might get fresh ideas on improving your product without infringement.

Using the **Patent Subscription Service** and establishing a deposit account with the Patent and Trademark Office, businesses can be sent full copies of all appropriate patents as they are issued. Selection is made using any of the more than 112,000 subclasses.

Contact: Patent and Trademark Office, Department of Commerce, Attn: Vangard Technologies Corporation, 14th & Constitution Avenue NW, Room 1627,

Washington, DC 20231. Phone Robert Sardelli at (202) 377-2481.

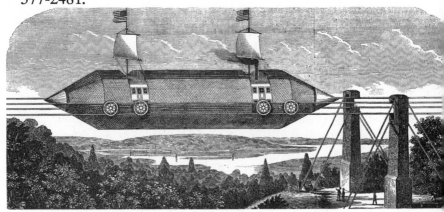

5. HOW TO FILE FOR A PATENT

The **Patent and Trademark Office** examines patent applications and grants protection for qualified inventions. It also collects, assembles, and disseminates the technological information disclosed on patent grants.

Printed copies of individual patents may be purchased directly from PTO. Printed collections of all new patents are issued each week in the Official Gazette which is available by subscription from the Government Printing Office.

A booklet, *General Information Concerning Patents*, is available from the Superintendent of Documents, Washington, DC 20202 for $2. An information booklet, *Basic Facts About Patents*, is available from the Patent Office.

Contact: Public Affairs Office, Patent and Trademark Office, Department of Commerce, Washington, DC 20231. Phone (703) 557-5168.

6. REGISTERING A TRADEMARK

Businesses interested in registering a trademark may contact this office for the information and forms required.

An information booklet, *Basic Facts About Trademarks*, is available.

Applications for trademark registration must be filed in the name of the owner of the mark. The owner may file his own application for registration, or he may be represented by an attorney.

Contact: Trademark Information, Patent and Trademark Office, Department of Commerce, Washington, DC 20231. Phone (703) 557-4636.

7. OBTAINING A COPYRIGHT

A series of pamphlets and forms is available to assist firms in understanding, searching, or applying for a copyright. Although the office cannot give legal advice, it can assist in providing information on claiming a copyright, what can be copyrighted, notice of copyright, transfer of a copyright, and searching records of the Copyright Office.

Contact: Copyright Office, Library of Congress, Washington, DC 20559. Phone (202) 479-0700.

8. WHERE TO GET INFORMATION ON FOREIGN RESEARCH

Technology-oriented businesses interested in staying up to date with foreign government technology will find the efforts of the **Foreign Technology Program** of special value. NTIS maintains formal agreements with more than 90 foreign sources of technical reports. In addition, NTIS receives foreign technical reports collected by other U.S. Government agencies. In all, some 20,000 foreign reports are annually added to the NTIS report collection.

A weekly newsletter provides useful information gathered from embassy and other sources around the world. Included in the newsletter are abstracts to the current foreign R&D results.

The countries covered by this program include Austria, Australia, Belgium, Canada, Denmark, Finland, France, Germany (FRG), Israel, Japan, the Netherlands, New Zealand, Norway, South Africa, Sweden, Switzerland, and the United Kingdom. Most of the reports from these countries are available in English.

Contact: Foreign Technology Program, National Technical Information Service (NTIS), Department of Commerce, 5285 Port Royal Road, Room 306F, Springfield, VA 22161. Phone (703) 487-4820.

9. HOW TO DEVELOP AND BRING A NEW PRODUCT TO MARKET

The Departments of Energy and Commerce, the National Society of Professional Engineers, the National Congress of Inventor Organizations, the Licensing Executives Society, and the American Intellectual Property Law Association sponsor two day seminars throughout the U.S.

The topics covered are; patenting and protection, estimating the worth of an invention, licensing, marketing, new business start-up, the business plan, research and development, venture financing, and the Department of Energy's Inventions Program and Small Business Innovative Research Programs.

If the new product is energy related, the Department of Energy may provide assistance in developing, financing, and marketing the product.

The seminar applies to all products, whether or not they're energy related.

To get more information, contact: Office of Energy-Related Inventions, National Institute of Standards and Technology (formerly National Bureau of Standards), Building 202, Room 209, Gaithersburg, MD 20899. Phone (301) 975-5500.

10. HELP TO STIMULATE THE INNOVATIVE PROCESS

The **Small Business Technology Liaison Division** and the Industrial Technology Partnership Division work with smaller firms to assist them to better understand the components of the innovative process. They focus on a company's understanding of business tools such as sensitivity analysis, technology screening, and networking resources. They can connect you with other groups involved in innovation.

Training is also provided in R&D (innovation) financing mechanisms and in the innovation process. Training, for individuals and small groups, is customized to requester's needs. It covers: innovation policy; cooperative and joint R&D arrangements; R&D limited partnerships; corporate partnering; Federal and National R&D funding; sources of cooperation between universities and industry; venture capital; and innovation facilitators. A series of special publications is available.

Contact: Office of Productivity, Technology, and Innovation, Department of Commerce, Room 4816, 14th & Constitution Avenue, NW, Washington DC 20230. Phone Lansing R. Felker at (202) 377-0940.

11. STUFF MADE OUT OF WOOD

It may surprise some to find that the Forest Service actively works with the private sector to develop new wood products for commercial use.

Their **Forest Products Laboratory** (FPL) in Madison, Wisconsin has developed such things as the **Truss-Framed System**, an innovative way to build homes and light commercial buildings. The system uses 30% less structural framing than conventional construction, can be put up faster by fewer people, and is more disaster resistant. Builders can expect about a 10-percent savings in construction costs.

It has been used in 31 states so far and its use is spreading rapidly as word spreads. The system has been assigned a public patent and can be used by anyone.

A more recent development is a **lightweight structural fiber panel** called FPL Spaceboard, which is molded from forest products. It is thinner, lighter and stronger than existing fiber boards. It may be used for lightweight containers or wall sections in houses, mobile homes, and recreational vehicles.

The Forest Products Laboratory has publications and experts on furniture manufacturing (including how to build a solar kiln for small custom furniture makers), box, pallet and crate packaging design, glues and glue products, manufacturing fuel for automobiles from forest waste, finishing wood exteriors, and fire retardants, plus many others.

If you have a sawmill, they can give your mill a tuneup that generally yields a 6-15% increase in efficiency and volume. They have publications helpful to lumber retailers, architects, builders and construction engineers.

For more information, write or call Colleen Morfoot, Information Specialist, Forest Products Laboratory, One Gifford Pinchot Drive, Madison, WI 53705-2398. Telephone (608) 231-9240.

12. A FACTORY OF THE FUTURE

The Center for Manufacturing Engineering operates the **Automated Manufacturing Research Facility** (AMRF). The main purposes are to address two basic problems in computer-integrated manufacturing:

(1) provide assurance that small firms will be able to obtain equipment from different manufacturers at different times and have them all work together without expensive custom-designed interfaces.

(2) find means of controlling quality in a fully automated factory by innovative measurement processes.

Dozens of companies, large and small, have sent their researchers to work in this facility beside their government counterparts. The results have been voluntary standards that are solving the compatibility problem.

In addition, over 36 patents, products, and systems have found their way into commercial use as a result of work at the AMRF.

All machines and computer systems used in the AMRF are made in the U.S. It is expected that 100,000 machine shops, mostly small, will take advantage of this automation technology.

As we are all aware, the U.S. has suffered on quality of manufacture products in the last two decades. AMRF techniques are revolutionizing the manufacturing process to make sure parts are made right the first time and every time. All this is accomplished with less waste, faster, with a set-up time of nearly zero.

Tours may be arranged through this exemplary facility in Gaithersburg, Maryland. Contact: Center for Manufacturing Engineering, Automated Manufacturing Research Facility, National Institute of Standards and Technology (formerly National Bureau of Standards), Gaithersburg, MD 20899. Phone Adrian Moll at (301) 975-6504.

Chapter 4

SELLING TO THE FEDS
(OR HOW TO GET YOUR
TAX MONEY BACK)

Uncle Sam can be your best customer; there is no product or service that he doesn't purchase someplace. One of the following should help:

1. BUSINESS SERVICE CENTERS

Business Service Centers (BSC) provide advice and counsel to those wishing to contract with the General Services Agency (GSA) or other agencies. GSA Business Service Centers (BSC) have been established to provide advice and counsel to business persons who are interested in contracting with GSA and other Federal agencies and departments. There are 13 centers nationwide, most of them located in GSA regional headquarters cities. Knowledgeable business counselors, trained to answer all but the most technical questions, are available. Often, BSC personnel are the first direct contact a business representative has with the Federal Government.

BSCs exist primarily to serve entrepreneurs in their search for Government contracts. BSC counselors provide individuals and firms with detailed information about all types of Government contracting opportunities. Copies of bid abstracts, which indicate names of successful bidders, other bidders, and price bids, are available in the centers. Information regarding the total dollar volume of GSA store stock items and quantity of items sold is also available.

These centers are responsible for issuing bidder's mailing list applications, furnishing invitations for bids and specifications to prospective bidders, maintaining a current display of bidding opportunities, safeguarding bids, providing bid-opening facilities, and furnishing free copies of publications designed to assist business representatives in doing business with the Federal Government.

BCSs also play an important role in the GSA's small business set-aside program and the small and disadvantaged business subcontracting programs. Check Appendix 3 to locate your nearest BSC or call (202) 566-1021.

2. SELLING CUPS AND SOCKS
AND ANTIQUE CLOCKS

If you have a common-use item for sale, while at the BSC ask for the **Public Liaison** staff.

The staff works with suppliers of common-use items and non-personal services for Federal agencies. Examples of items include: office supplies and equipment, furniture, tools, hardware, refrigerators, air-conditioners, water coolers, scientific and laboratory equipment, medical, photographic, and audio-video recording equipment and supplies. The various programs under which procurements are made are described in the following sections.

Stock Program: Under this program, a wide variety of common-use items are stored in supply facilities located nationwide for timely and cost-effective distribution to customer agencies.

Federal Supply Schedules: This program provides Federal agencies with sources for products and services such as furniture, electric lamps, appliances, photographic, duplicating, athletic, laboratory, and audio and video recording equipment and supplies. Schedules are indefinite quantity contracts entered into with commercial firms to provide supplies and services at stated prices for given periods of time. They permit agencies to place orders directly with suppliers. Federal supply schedules are published to provide ordering data for these contracts.

Special Order Program: Items sometimes are not suitable for inclusion in either the stock or Federal supply schedule programs. Agency requirements for such items are consolidated by GSA and special definite quantity contracts are executed. Direct delivery is made from the contractor to the agency involved. Information is available on supplying items for these programs and placement on a bidders mail list.

3. PASS: HOW TO GET EASY EXPOSURE FOR YOUR PRODUCTS AND CAPABILITIES TO ALL GOVERNMENT AGENCIES

You just fill out one simple form that takes about five minutes to complete. At your SBA office (this form is available at many other offices also) ask for **PASS**

(**Procurement Automated Source System**) information. This automated system substantially improves government contract and subcontract opportunities for small businesses.

Through PASS, a company becomes part of a nation-wide government agency resource list utilized by head-quarter and field procurement offices in the matching of many procurement requirements against capabilities in the PASS database. Major Federal prime contractors also use PASS to identify subcontracting opportunities. The system is based upon the use of selected key words.

4. PROCUREMENT DATA

Contact the **Federal Procurement Data Center** in Washington to get procurement information customized for your needs. The center is a unique source of consolidated information about Federal purchases; its information can assist businesses in their planning and marketing efforts. A master database contains detailed information on the purchases by more than sixty agencies. Companies can learn how much the Government spent in each fiscal quarter on items such as clothing, food, furniture, fuel, building materials, ADP services, and weapons.

Two types of reports are available. A free standard report contains statistical procurement information in snapshot form. It also compares procurement activities by state, major product and service codes, degree of competition, and contractors.

Special reports tailored to a specific need are also available. They can be based upon up to 25 data elements which can be cross-tabulated in hundreds of ways. Such a report can help analyze Government procurement data and trends, identify competitors, and locate Federal markets for individual products or services.

Information can include name of Federal agency purchasing offices, product or service and date an agreement was reached, contractor's name and address, dollar amount obligated, extent of competition, and type of business that received an award.

Examples of previously requested topics include: who purchased and sold traffic signal systems; contracts awarded to specific companies for IBM compatibles; awards to a specific corporation; construction contracting by state; contract awards for specific counties or states; the top 300 contractors of DOD for R & D contracts; and the top 200 product codes ranked by dollars awarded.

On a reimbursable basis, the center will also provide computer tapes of the entire contents of its database; mailing lists of contractors who sell to the Government sorted by region, product, and service code, etc. and mailing lists of Government purchasing offices.

Call or write: General Services Administration, 4040 N. Fairfax Ave., Suite 900, Arlington, VA 22203. Phone (703) 235-1326.

5. WHO WANTS WHAT COMPUTER

Contact the **Federal Equipment Data Center** if your specialty is computer-related. The center maintains a Government-wide inventory of all owned and leased general purpose data processing equipment, provided these system components exceed a purchase value of $50,000 or a monthly rental value of $1,667.

Information collected includes the make, model, and manufacturer of each component; the acquisition cost; the agency using the equipment, and the projected date of replacement or upgrade. This information is received from more than 60 Federal departments and agencies, and forms the database for the Automatic Data Processing Equipment Data System (ADPE/DS).

This unique data system provides a consolidated source of information about Federal ADP equipment inventory. The available data can be used to analyze where and when large ADP replacement or upgrade may occur, what types of equipment will be involved, where compatible installations are located, and the location of leased equipment.

This information can be a powerful marketing tool. The information is accessible through two types of reports.

The ADPE/DS standard report is issued semi-annually and contains statistics and graphics pertaining to manufacturer's market share, age of the inventory, agency inventories, dollar share, and component mix. Special reports, tailored to an individual's data needs, also are available for a nominal charge.

The special reports are available on a reimbursable basis. They can be tailored to a specific need and can be formatted in any way the requestor desires. Information such as the make, model, and manufacturer of the equipment, the city and state where the equipment is located, the equipment's age, whether it is leased or owned, and the planned upgrade dates can be sorted and analyzed.

Call or write: General Services Administration, WKHE, 4040 N. Fairfax, Suite 900, Arlington, VA 22203. Phone Ms. Louise Oliver at (703) 235-2870.

6. DOD POTENTIAL CONTRACTORS

If you want to try defense projects, join the **Potential Contractor Program**. The program was established to certify and register non-government organizations for access to Department of Defense scientific and technical information. This includes information on needs, requirements, work, and accomplishments associated with research, development, test, and evaluation. Through this program, organizations are provided the opportunity and means to obtain current scientific and technical information required to maintain their capabilities as developers and producers of military equipment and materials. Firms, individuals, or activities with a demonstrable capability of performing research/development with a reasonable potential for eventually receiving a contract with DOD are invited to participate in the program.

Contact: Department of Defense, Tri-Service Industry Information Centers, 5001 Eisenhower Avenue, Alexandria, VA 22333-0001. Phone (202) 274-8948 for the

Army, (202) 274-9305 for the Air Force, and (202) 274-9315 for the Navy.

7. BECOME CERTIFIED AS "COMPETENT" THROUGH THE CERTIFICATE OF COMPETENCY PROGRAM

The program will certify a small company's capability, competency, credit, integrity, perseverance and tenacity to perform a specific government contract. If a Federal contracting officer proposes to reject the bid of a small business firm which is a low bidder because he questions the firm's ability to perform the contract on any of the above grounds, the case is referred to SBA. SBA personnel then contact the company concerned to inform it of the impending decision, and to offer an opportunity to apply to SBA for a **Certificate of Competency (COC)**, which, if granted, would require award of the contract to the firm in accordance with the Small Business Act.

SBA may also, at its discretion, issue a COC in connection with the sale of Federal property if the responsibility (capacity, credit, integrity, tenacity and perseverance) of the purchaser is questioned, and for firms found ineligible by a contracting officer due to a provision of the Walsh-Healey Public Contracts Act which requires that a government contractor be either a manufacturer or a regular dealer.

Contact: Industrial Assistance Office, Small Business Administration, Room 600, 1441 L Street, NW, Washington, DC 20416. Phone (202) 653-6582.

8. FOR MORE INFORMATION ON SELLING TO SPECIFIC AGENCIES

Department of Agriculture

Procurement procedures are explained in *Selling to USDA*. This publication contains information on who does the buying, the types of items bought for the various programs, and where the buying is done. Included is a directory of purchasing offices and their locations.

Copies are available from: Department of Agriculture, Procurement Division, Room 1550, South Bldg., Washington, DC 20215. Phone (202) 447-7527.

Department of Commerce

Procurement procedures are explained in *How to Sell to the Department of Commerce*. This publication contains information on who-buys-what-where. Included is a directory of purchasing offices and their locations.

Copies are available from: General Procurement Division, Department of Commerce, 14th & Constitution Avenue NW, Room H6517, Washington, DC 20230. Phone (202) 377-5555.

Department of Defense

The Economic Adjustment Office assists state and local governments in helping their area's businesses sell to the Department of Defense (DOD). They have a special report titled *Defense Procurement and Economic Development*, which overviews the DOD procurement systems and provides information about the many special publications available to help businesses in the procurement process. Although this publication is targeted to government users, businesses will find it useful in learning about Defense business opportunities.

Contact: Economic Adjustment Office, Department of Defense, Room 4C161 Pentagon, Washington, DC 20301-4000. Phone (202) 697-0041.

Department of Energy

The Procurement Operations Office handles acquisitions, grants, cooperative agreements, loan guarantees and other financial assistance instruments, management and operating contracts, personal property management, sales contracts, small business/small disadvantaged business/labor surplus area acquisitions, and other business activities.

The procurement procedures of the Department are explained in *Doing Business with the Department of Energy*. This publication contains information on who does the buying, the types of items, and where the buying is done. Included is a directory of purchasing offices and their locations.

Copies are available from: Department of Energy, Procurement and Assistance Management Directorate, Code: MA 451, 1000 Independence Ave. SW, Washington, DC 20585. Phone (202) 586-8201.

Department of Housing and Urban Development

Doing Business with HUD explains HUD's mission, major programs and the procurement opportunities it creates, both directly through HUD and indirectly through State and local governments and other organizations which receive financial assistance from the Department.

Also included is a brief description of HUD's procurement procedures, a directory of purchasing offices, and an explanation of HUD's Procurement Opportunity Programs for minority, women-owned businesses.

Copies are available from: Procurement and Contracts Office, Department of Housing and Urban Development, Room 5260, 451 Seventh Street SW, Washington, DC 20410. Phone (202) 755-5294.

Environmental Protection Agency

The procurement procedures are explained in *Doing Business with EPA*. This booklet will aid a business in its efforts to acquire contract work with EPA. It contains information on contact points, addresses and telephone numbers of contracting offices, and describes the types of products and services generally acquired of EPA.

Contact: Environmental Protection Agency, Washington, DC 20460. Phone (202) 475-9428.

Department of the Treasury

The procurement procedures are explained in *Selling to the Department of the Treasury*. This publication contains information on who does the buying, the types of items bought for the various programs, and where the buying is done. Included is a directory of purchasing offices and their locations.

Copies are available from Department of Treasury, Room 1458 Treasury Building, Washington, DC 20220. Phone (202) 566-2586.

Veterans Administration

Request *Could You Use a Multibillion Dollar Customer?* which has everything you need to know about this lucrative market.

Contact: Procurement and Supply Services Office, Veterans Administration, 810 Vermont Avenue NW (93), Washington, DC 20420. Phone (202) 233-3054.

Chapter 5

ABOUT SHIPPING

1. UNCLE SAM HELPS NEGOTIATE WITH TRANSPORTATION FIRMS

The **Transportation Office** helps small grain cooperatives and merchandising firms negotiate rate and service conditions with railroads. The office publishes a weekly Grain Transportation Report to keep small shippers apprised of changes in grain transportation and also offers technical assistance and advice for specific transportation-related problems.

Contact: Railroad Department, Transportation Office, Department of Agriculture, 14th & Independence Avenue SW, Washington, DC 20250. Phone (202) 653-6157.

2. SENDING PERISHABLES OVERSEAS.

Most perishable agricultural commodities move into the export market by air or ocean transportation. **The Transportation Office** assists exporters with ocean and air freight transportation problems through a liaison with major transportation companies, shipping agencies, regulatory bodies, and foreign agricultural attaches.

Technical assistance and information is available to small businessmen who encounter exportation problems. Specific information on the transportation requirements for exporting produce is available in two handbooks. Tip sheets on the transportation of livestock are available. In addition, short-term applied research conducted on special problems encountered in the transport of agricultural products is available.

Contact: Export Shipping Department, Transportation Office, Department of Agriculture, 14th & Independence Avenue SW, Washington, DC 20250. Phone (202) 653-6275.

3. HELP WITH OCEAN COMMON CARRIERS

The **Federal Maritime Commission** provides a forum for settling disputes between carriers and shippers. The Commission will listen to informal complaints and try to bring about a voluntary settlement. If warranted, formal proceedings can be initiated for unlawful practices. They may award reparations for economic injuries from violations.

In 1987 they responded to 1,086 inquiries and complaints.

Contact: Office of Informal Complaints and Inquiries, Federal Maritime Commission, 1100 L Street NW, Washington, DC 20573. Phone Joe Farrell, Director at (202) 523-5807.

4. TRUCK COSTS AND TECHNICAL HELP

Many truckers of agricultural commodities are also small businessmen in that they use their own tractor and trailer to haul freight for a profit. For these small owner-operators, the **Transportation Office** publishes a monthly truck cost report, which provides information on current per-mile operating costs for a typical fresh fruit and vegetable trucker. Information on this report, as well as technical assistance for individual truckers, is available.

Contact: Truck Department, Transportation Office, Department of Agriculture, P.O. Box 96575, Washington, DC 20090. Phone (202) 653-6206.

5. PROBLEMS TO AVOID IF YOU'RE STARTING A TRUCKING COMPANY

The **Public Assistance Office** acts as a clearinghouse and focal point for the resolution of questions and problems experienced by businesses and individuals. It provides advice and technical assistance to small businesses, minority truckers, new entrants into the transportation field, small shippers, and small carriers, and deals with other members of the general public as well.

Its chief function is to counsel small business entities and individuals in understanding and coping with the rules, regulations, policies, and procedures of the Commission. Much of this work involves assistance in obtaining operating rights — licenses to perform interstate transportation — from how to fill out the application form to complying with tariff filings and insurance requirements.

As part of its information outreach program, the office prepares and disseminates numerous booklets designed to answer some basic questions about the surface transportation industries. These include problems small businesses and individuals confront in entering the trucking business, starting a short-line railroad, and participating in rail abandonment proceedings.

The office plays a significant role in tackling and preventing transportation problems by initiating or commenting upon proposed rules or legislation relating to matters impacting upon areas of concern to small businesses.

Contact: Public Assistance Office, Interstate Commerce Commission, Washington, DC 20423. Phone (202) 275-7597.

6. SO YOU WANT TO START
A SMALL RAILROAD

It may surprise some to find out the short-line railroad industry is experiencing a comeback. In 1987, 51 new owners or operators were authorized to begin operation. One reason is the Interstate Commerce Commission's refusal to burden new operators with the cost of labor-protective conditions. Write for a copy of *So You Want To Start a Small Railroad* from the Office of Public Assistance, Interstate Commerce Commission, Washington, DC 20423, or call Fran Grimmett at (202) 275-7597.

Chapter 6

EVERYTHING YOU EVER WANTED TO KNOW, BUT WERE ASHAMED TO ASK (OR QUESTIONS THAT WOULD MAKE DR. RUTH BLUSH)

1. CUSTOMIZED ECONOMIC RESEARCH

Customized data is available from an economic model designed to measure the impacts of private sector developments and of government programs. Some of the variables included are output, employment, wage rates, population, government revenues, retail sales, investment, and labor force. The model can be used to analyze regional distribution of policy or economic impacts. It assures that the sum of regional activities is consistent with forecasts of national activity.

Businesses can also obtain special data showing the economic effects of potential projects on specific regions. The system offers estimates of economic impact multipliers for 500 industries for any county or group of counties in the United States.

Some examples of the use of the Regional Input-Output Modeling System include: determination of the effect that new warehouse construction would have on personal earnings, assessing the employment effects of various types of urban redevelopment expenditures, the economic impact of port facility expansion, or the effects of new plants on regional private-sector economic activity.

Contact: Bureau of Economic Analysis, Department of Commerce, 1401 K Street, N.W., Washington, DC 20230. Phone Dr. John Kort at (202) 523-0591 for state and national impact and phone (202) 523-0594 for analysis by county.

2. CORRECT IN EVERY WEIGH

The **Weights and Measures Office** provides leadership and technical resources to assure that commercial weights and measures are accurate and that quantity statements on packages are correct. It promotes a uniform national weights and measures system and sponsors the **National Conference on Weights and Measures** as a national forum for the promotion of uniformity and effectiveness in state and local weights and measures programs.

Data is prepared and distributed on weights and measures units, systems, and equivalents for use by

Federal, state and local governments, educational institutions, business and industry, and the general public.

Contact: Weights and Measures Office, National Institute of Standards and Technology (formerly National Bureau of Standards), Department of Commerce, Room A-617, Gaithersburg, MD 20899. Phone (301) 975-4009.

3. BUSINESS STATISTICS 24 HOURS A DAY, 365-1/4 DAYS A YEAR

Four special telephone lines allow businesses to call any hour of the day to get recorded information on major economic statistics. The index of leading indicators recording includes the levels and percentage changes for the latest three months for the leading indicators. Also included are the contribution that changes in each of the dozen statistical series made to the overall index.

Another recording provides details on the latest quarterly survey of business intentions to invest in new plants and equipment. This telephone line also carries information on two other quarterly statistics, merchandise trade on a balance of payments basis and U.S. international transactions.

A third number handles the Gross National Product figures. The so-called "flash estimate" for the current quarter figures is covered.

Details of personal income and outlays are available on the fourth telephone line.

Call (202) 898-2450 for a recording of the leading indicator statistics; 898-2453 for new plant and equipment investment statistics; 898-2451 for gross national product statistics; and 898-2452 for personal income and outlay statistics. 202-219-0515

If you need to write them, it's: Bureau of Economic Analysis, Department of Commerce, Room BE-53, 1401 K Street NW, Washington, DC 20230.

4. USING CENSUS DATA TO LOCATE YOUR BUSINESS OR CUSTOMERS

Owners and operators of small businesses often find statistics from the Census Bureau to be of value in such activities as selecting the best location for a new store, deciding on target areas for advertising, determining an appropriate share of the market, and assessing business competition. Census statistics contribute to planning and decision making in these activities through helping business people determine how many potential customers there are in an area, what the dollar value of sales is in merchandise lines of interest to them, what volume of business is done by specific types of businesses, and the answers to related questions.

Included in Census Bureau reports are statistics showing the number of people in defined areas by age, race, sex, occupation, income, and other characteristics; the number of households and selected housing information, including housing value and rent; business activity and industrial production; imports/exports, and other useful information.

Data from the censuses are generally presented for cities, metropolitan areas, counties, states, regions, and the nation. In addition, the Census of Population and Housing is the source of data for much smaller areas, such as city blocks and census tracts (small areas roughly equivalent to neighborhoods).

Contact: Bureau of the Census, Department of Commerce, Customer Service Branch, Washington, DC 20233. Phone (301) 763-4100. Regional Census offices also may be contacted for assistance.

5. FEDERAL HELP ON AUTOMATING YOUR BUSINESS

A critical element of the U.S. industrial base, both civilian and military, is the 130,000 small manufacturing

firms which have traditionally supplied 70% of the component parts to our largest manufacturers. They are under intense competitive pressure from overseas suppliers.

The elements of that competition they must contend with are:

1) world-class quality,
2) price,
3) just-in-time delivery
4) rapid response to changing market needs and new technologies.

The challenges small manufacturing businesses face are that:

1) most do not truly understand that they are competing in global markets,

2) they do not know about off-the-shelf Flexible Computer Integrated Manufacturing (FCIM) systems which offer one key potential solution. FCIM provides small batch production of a wide variety of products, with almost no down time, with the same per-unit cost for batches of 1 or 1,000,

3) many small firm owners are not computer literate and so are afraid of FCIM,

4) the cost can be prohibitive for an individual firm attempting to adopt FCIM,

5) most CEOs do not know how to manage a firm using FCIM as a tool in a total business context.

To help small firms cope with these problems, the Department of Commerce's Office of Productivity, Technology, and Innovation developed a business financing/management/transition technique called shared FCIM. This consists of a manufacturing service center which has state-of-the-art/off-the-shelf Flexible Manufacturing Systems (FMS) systems that lease manufacturing time to small firms.

This is the same technique used by main-frame computer manufacturers to introduce computers to the business community in the 1950s. However, it became clear that retraining of management and work whether it was leased or used in-house, that FCIM must be understood in a total business context.

The result was the development of the "Teaching Factory" which combines the manufacturing service center and a comprehensive educational component for management and workforce.

The resulting benefits include: immediate competitive manufacturing capability with no large up-front costs, strategic planning for the appropriate degree of automation, training of management and workforce before making an investment, testing of systems to assure they meet individual firm needs and fast utilization of capacity when firms install their own equipment.

Currently, projects call for the first center to be in pilot operation in January 1989, a second in March 1989. A third plans to begin operation in September 1989. Two additional centers are scheduled to begin operations in 1990. Some five others are in active initial planning and 15 additional groups are beginning initial consideration.

A short mention of the program in the *Kiplinger Washington Letter* resulted in 450 requests for information. Based on the projections of the centers beginning implementation or planning some 200 shared FCIMs are envisioned in the next decade.

Key points to remember are that:

1) Flexible manufacturing automation may well be critical to the survival of many domestic small manufacturing businesses.

2) Only a small percentage of small firms have begun to automate — most without a long-term strategy.

3) Management understanding of the true **business impact** of automation is key to its **adoption** and **effective use**.

Contact: Office of Productivity, Technology and Innovation, U.S. Department of Commerce, Room 4816, Washington, DC 20230. Phone Theodore J. Lettes at (202) 377-5804.

6. MANUFACTURING CENTERS

The Manufacturing Technology Centers Program helps small- and medium-size companies implement automated manufacturing technology. The **National Institute of Standards and Technology** (formerly National Bureau of Standards) provides planning and operating funds to the centers, along with participation in cooperative exchanges of modern technology. Advanced manufacturing techniques and methods for fostering their use that are successful at one center are generally for use in the centers and businesses throughout the nation.

Contact: Manufacturing Technology Centers Program, National Institute of Standards and Technology (formerly National Bureau of Standards), Department of Commerce, Building 220, Room A319, Gaithersburg, MD 20899. Phone (301) 975-5020.

7. FLEXIBLE MANUFACTURING SYSTEMS PROGRAM

This program provides basic data on concepts related to financing methods and organizational structures that can make automation a realistic option for small- and medium-sized manufacturers. Information is provided on computer-integrated manufacturing, and especially on automated, flexible manufacturing systems. They will consult with you on your problem.

Contact: Flexible Manufacturing Systems Program, Office of Productivity, Technology and Innovation, Department of Commerce, 14th & E Street NW, Room 4814B, Washington, DC 20230. Phone (202) 377-5804.

8. EASY ACCESS TO PRICE AND COST DATA

Information is available which helps evaluate consumer, producer, export, and import prices and price changes. **The Bureau of Labor Statistics** provides the actual data and assistance in using this data for two major economic indexes: the consumer price index (CPI) and the producer price index (PPI).

A series of regularly issued publications is prepared by this office. The major titles are *Consumer Price Index*, *Producer Price Index*, *Export Price Index*, and *Import Price Index*.

Recorded messages offer: General CPI and employment data (202) 523-9658; Detailed CPI data (202) 523-1239; Detailed produce price data (202) 523-1765; and Detailed employment data (202) 523-1944.

Contact: Bureau of Labor Statistics, Department of Labor, 600 E Street NW, Room 3205, Washington, DC 20212. To talk to Homo Sapiens call (202) 272-5038.

9. PRODUCTIVITY INDEXES FOR
YOUR INDUSTRY

Indexes of productivity for more than 150 industries are published each year. The factors underlying productivity movements also are carried out. Comparison of U.S. and foreign productivity are available. Comparative productivity measures for the total economy and the iron and steel industry and other labor economic indicators — hourly compensation costs, unit labor costs, prices, employment and unemployment, industrial dispute activity, and other selected measures are prepared.

Employment and occupational implications of technological change and technological changes emerging among selected American industries and the technological innovations such as computers are available. In addition, in-depth studies are prepared periodically for selected major industries where significant changes are taking place on a large scale.

Contact: Bureau of Labor Statistics, Department of Labor, Francis Perkins Building S-4325, 200 Constitution Avenue NW, Washington, DC 20210. Phone Edward Dean at (202) 523-9294.

10. FINDING OUT HOW YOU COMPARE WITH
THE COMPETITION

The **Interfirm Productivity Comparisons** (IPC) program is a method for a group of managers of competing firms in the same industry to receive confidential productivity report cards based on a set of approximately 30 critical operating and financial ratios. Participants also receive numerical class ranks describing how their firm compares with competitors.

In addition, organizations sponsoring interfirm comparisons projects (e.g. trade associations) are given summary analyses useful for policy or program initiatives in behalf of the industry.

The **Office of Productivity** offers technical assistance, explanations of the concept, and basic information a prospective user needs before undertaking an **Interfirm Productivity Comparison**. This OPTI service is provided to groups of companies principally through such intermediary vehicles as trade associations.

Contact: Interfirm Productivity Comparisons Program, Office of Productivity, Technology, and Innovation, Department of Commerce, Room 4814B, 14th & E Street NW, Washington, DC 20230. Phone (202) 377-2922.

11. INFORMATION ON RADIO, TV AND TELECOMMUNICATIONS

The office of **Policy Analysis and Development** will assist businesses in locating information or assistance concerning the deregulation of telecommunications industries, the telephone industry, radio and television broadcasting, and cable television. It also assists in linking businesses to appropriate telecommunications contacts.

Contact: Office of Policy Analysis and Development, National Telecommunications and Information Administration, Department of Commerce, 14th & Constitution Avenue NW, Room 4725, Washington, DC 20230. Phone (202) 377-1800.

12. UNCLE SAM WILL HELP YOU LEARN JAPANESE MANAGEMENT TECHNIQUES (PLUS OTHER HOT TIPS FOR PRODUCTIVITY)

The **Commerce Productivity Center** provides information on how to improve business productivity. Topics covered: productivity management; productivity improvement methods; productivity measurement; quality of working life; labor-management cooperation; white collar productivity; quality improvement; motivation; new technologies for factories and offices; Japanese management techniques; company improvement experiences; technology and innovation; productivity in government; industry productivity; and productivity in the economy.

The Center's reference room is open to the public. A variety of private and public sector publications, articles, reference/referral services, bibliographies, and reading lists on numerous productivity are available.

Contact: Commerce Productivity Center, Office of Productivity, Technology, and Innovation, Department of Commerce, Room 7413, 14th & E Street NW, Washington, DC 20230. Phone Carol Ann Meares at (202) 377-0940.

13. MAKE USE OF FEDERAL COMPUTERIZED INFORMATION SEARCHES

Information searches tailored for your needs are available from the **Industrial Applications Centers**. Two types of literature searches are offered:

(1) Retrospective Searches identify published or unpublished literature. Results are screened and documents identified according to a client's interest profile. Results are tailored to specific needs. Backup reports identified in a search usually are available upon request.

(2) Current Awareness Searches provide selected weekly, monthly, or quarterly abstracts on new developments in any selected area of interest. Companies will receive printouts automatically.

Technical assistance is also available. IAC engineers will help evaluate the results of these literature searches. They can find answers to technical problems and put clients in touch with scientists and engineers at appropriate NASA Field Centers.

Prospective clients can obtain more information about these services by contacting the nearest center. User fees are charged for their information services. The seven centers are:

(1) Aerospace Research Applications Center, Indianapolis Center for Advanced Research, 611 N. Capitol Avenue, Indianapolis, IN 46204. Phone (317) 262-5003.

(2) Kerr Industrial Applications Center, Southeastern Oklahoma State University, Station A, Box 2584, Durant, OK 74701. Phone (405) 924-6822.

(3) NASA Industrial Applications Center, 823 William Pitt Union, University of Pittsburgh, Pittsburgh, PA 15260. Phone (412) 624-5211.

(4) NASA Industrial Applications Center, University of Southern California, Denney Research Building, Los Angeles, CA 90007. Phone (213) 743-6132.

(5) NASA-Florida State Technology Applications Center, University of Florida, 307 Weil Hall, Gainesville, FL 32611. Phone (904) 392-6760.

(6) NASA/UK Technology Applications Program, University of Kentucky, 109 Kinkead Hall, Lexington, KY 40506. Phone (606) 257-6322.

(7) New England Research Applications Center, Mansfield Professional Park, Storrs, CT 06268. Phone (203) 486-4533.

14. BUSINESS DEVELOPMENT IN RURAL COMMUNITIES

ATTRA (Appropriate Technology Transfer for Rural Areas) is a Department of Agriculture Extension Service which provides technical assistance to farmers, agri-businessmen, horticultural operators, "hobby" farmers, and gardeners. They specialize in low input and sustainable agriculture (USA) techniques that minimize the need for off-farm purchase of items such as fertilizer and pesticides.

Businesses such as earthworm production, aquaculture, field-grown flowers, or farmers market start-ups have received information from ATTRA.

Information is available by calling their toll free number 1-800-346-9140. You may write them at ATTRA, P.O. Box 3657, Fayetteville, Arkansas 72702.

15. QUESTIONS ABOUT STANDARDS, SPECIFICATIONS, TEST METHODS AND NOMENCLATURE

The **National Center for Standards and Certification Information** maintains a reference collection on more than 240,000 standards, specifications, test methods, certification rules, codes, nomenclature, and recommended practices.

They can answer questions such as:

Are there standards for electric toasters?

Have test methods been established for characteristics of bricks?

Has nomenclature for quality control been defined?

Have specifications for magnetic ink been established?

They can answer the same questions for some foreign countries, or can refer you to the right person.

A newsletter is published on proposed U.S. or foreign regulations that may affect U.S. manufacturers.

Contact: National Center for Standards and Certification Information, Room A-629, Administration Building, National Institute of Standards and Technology (formerly Bureau of Standards), Gaithersburg, MD 20899. Phone (301) 975-4040.

16. ASSISTANCE FOR ENERGY-RELATED PROJECTS

The **National Appropriate Technology Assistance Service (NATAS)** helps entrepreneurs develop energy-related projects by providing information and direct business assistance. They can help with such things as: identifying the best opportunities, acquiring financing, marketing, business planning, and organization. Technical support on inventions is also provided.

One of the more innovative aspects of NATAS is its commercialization technical assistance.

Contact: NATAS, Department of Energy, P O Box 2525, Butte, MT 59702. Phone Jeff Birkby at (800) 428-2525, or in Montana (800) 428-1718.

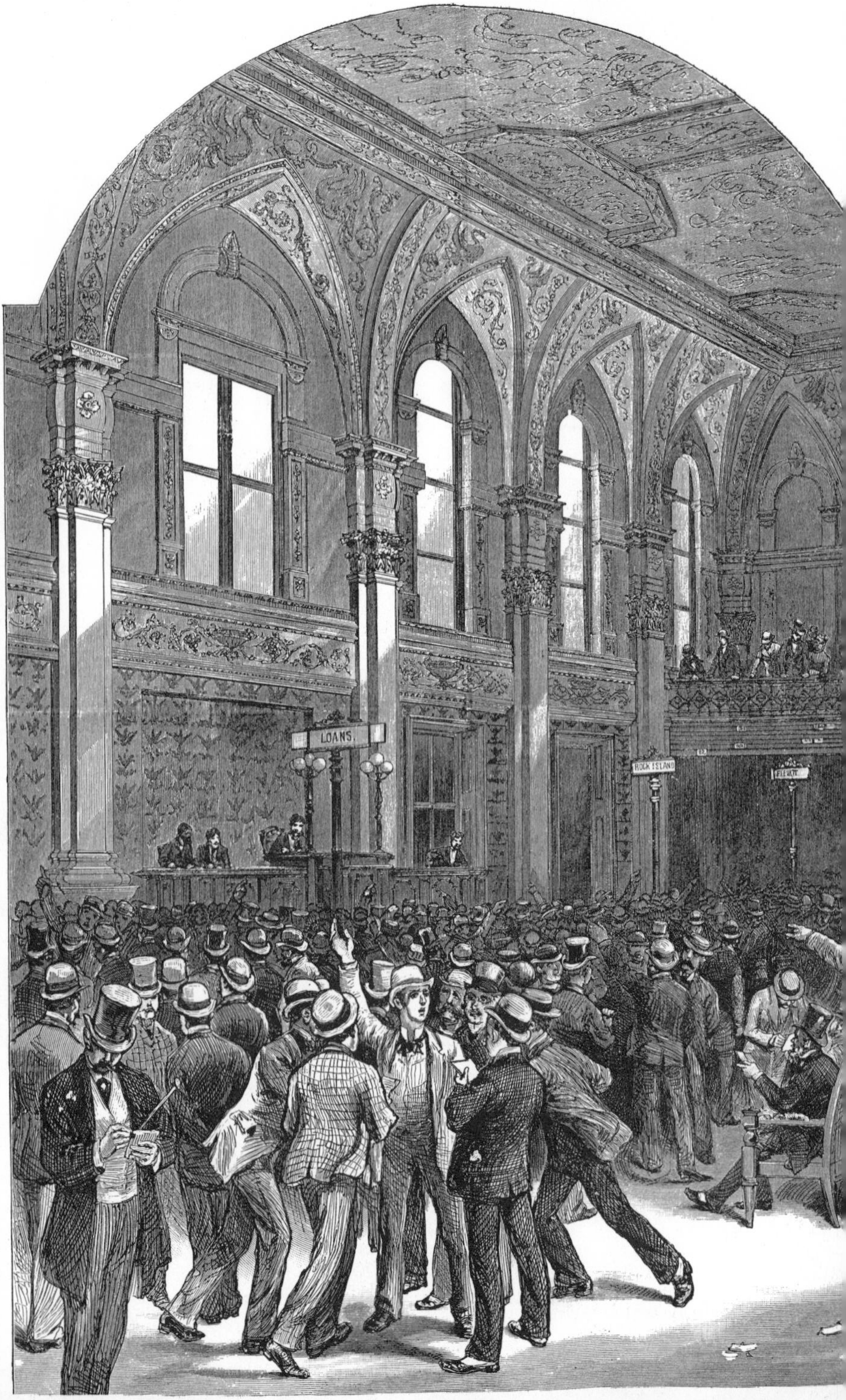
LOANS.
ROCK ISLAND

Chapter 7

FINANCIAL HELP

1. FINANCIAL LOANS FOR BUSINESS IN SMALL TOWNS

The Farmers Home Administration's **Business and Industrial Loan Program** guarantees up to 90% of principal and interest on loans made by commercial lenders to establish or improve businesses and industries, if they primarily are used to help preserve or create new employment opportunities for rural people. Loans may assist enterprises located in the countryside and intowns or cities of up to a population of 50,000.

The money may be used for business acquisitions, construction, conversion, enlargement, repair, purchasing land, easements, buildings, equipment and supplies.

The FmHA has fewer rules than the SBA; for example, the FmHA will consider loans for publishing enterprises and the SBA will (usually) not.

Contact: Farmers Home Administration, Department of Agriculture, 14th & Independence Avenue SW, Washington, DC 20250. Phone (202) 447-4323.

2. LOANS FOR TEENAGERS

Youth Project Loans from the **Farmers Home Administration** are available to youngsters ages 10 through 20 in rural communities. They will finance nearly any kind of income-producing project. Kids have started landscaping companies, repair shops, catering services, roadside stands and art/crafts sales enterprises, among others. The money can be used for equipment, supplies, renting tools, buying livestock, and for operating expenses. Only small projects are financed.

Contact: Youth Project Loans, Farmers Home Administration, 14th & Independence Avenue SW, Washington, DC 20250. For a pamphlet describing the program call (202) 382-1632.

3. NONFARM ENTERPRISES ON FARMS

The **Farmers Home Administration** makes loans and gives technical and management assistance for businesses to supplement farm income. They can make loans up to $200,000 and guarantee bank loans up to $400,000. These loans have financed welding shops, service stations, grocery stores, barber shops, cabinetmakers, sporting goods stores, beauty shops, riding stables, repair services, and restaurants, among others.

Applications of veterans receive preference. To be eligible one must be or intend to become the owner-operator of a family-sized farm or be a tenant on such a farm.

The loans may be used for buildings, land, buying or renting tools and equipment, furnishings, operating expenses, refinance debts, pay closing costs, purchase inventories or supplies, pay for organizing the enterprise, develop water and waste disposal systems for the enterprise and construct necessary roads.

Contact: Farmers Home Administration, 14th & Independence Avenue SW, Washington, DC 20250. Phone

(202) 447-4323 and ask for the Nonfarm Enterprise Loan pamphlet.

4. A POTPOURRI OF FARMERS HOME ADMINISTRATION LOANS

The FmHA has loan programs for purchasing and developing farms, buying livestock and equipment, paying farm and home operating equipment, converting farms to outdoor recreation enterprises, constructing buildings and homes, providing rental housing, developing water and waste disposal systems, refinancing debts, and soil and water conservation.

Contact: Farmers Home Administration, Department of Agriculture, 14th & Independence Avenue SW, Washington, DC 20250. Phone (202) 447-4323.

5. IF YOU HAVE A LOW INCOME OR HAVE BEEN DENIED FINANCING

If you have a low income, are located in a high unemployment area *or* have been denied financing despite ability to repay, the Small Business Administration may have a loan for you. Funds may be used to construct, expand or convert facilities, purchase equipment, or for working capital. In 1989 appeoximately 2 billion dollars will be available to fourteen thousand applicants thru direct loans or loan guarantees. Direct loans range up to $150,000, guarantees up to $500,000.

Ask for information on the 7(a) and 7(a)(11) programs.

Contact: Director, Office of Business Loans, Small Business Administration, 1441 L St. NW, Washington, DC 20416. Phone (202) 653-6470.

6. LOAN GUARANTEES FOR AGRICULTURAL EXPORTS

The **Export Credit Guarantee Program** (GSM-102) run by the **Agriculture Department's Commodity Credit Corporation** is designed to expand U.S. agricultural exports by stimulating U.S. bank financing of foreign purchases on credit terms of up to three years. In every transaction the foreign buyer's bank must issue an irrevocable letter of credit covering the port value of the commodity exported.

The **Credit Corporation's** guarantee will cover most of the amount owed to the U.S. bank in case the foreign bank defaults. The program operates in situations where credit is necessary to increase or maintain U.S. exports to a foreign market and where private financial institutions would be unwilling to provide financing without guarantee.

A secondary objective is to permit some countries with improved financial conditions to purchase on fully commercial terms.

The **Intermediate Export Credit Guarantee** program (GSM-103) is similar but provides coverage on credit terms in excess of three but not greater than ten years.

Under these programs, guarantee coverage may be made available on credits extended for freight cost and marine and war risk insurance costs associated with U.S. agricultural exports. The **Credit Corporation** announces availability of such coverage on a case-by-case basis.

Contact: Foreign Agricultural Service, Commodity Credit Corporation, Department of Agriculture, 14th & Independence Avenue SW, Washington, DC 20250. Phone (202) 447-3224.

7. GRANTS FOR INVENTIONS

The **Energy-Related Inventions Office** encourages innovation in non-nuclear energy technology by helping individual inventors and small R&D companies to develop

promising energy-related inventions. It evaluates all submitted inventions and recommends those that are promising, to the Department of Energy (DOE).

The evaluation criteria are: technical feasibility, degree
of energy impact, commercial potential, and intrinsic technical merit. DOE then reviews the recommended inventions and, working closely with the inventor, determines
the next reasonable step for the invention and how much
money it will take. Most often, support takes the form of a
one-time-only cash grant and technical assistance in
developing linkages with the private sector.

Contact: Energy-Related Inventions Office, National
Institute of Standards and Technology (formerly National
Bureau of Standards), Department of Commerce, Building
202, Room 209, Gaithersburg, MD 20899. Phone (301)
975-5500.

8. FUNDS FOR FISHING

The **Commercial Fisheries Financial Assistance Programs** include the:

1. **Fisheries Obligation Guarantee Program** which provides a Federal Guarantee of financing of commercial fishing vessels and shoreside facilities.

2. **Capital Construction Fund Program** which defers Federal income taxes for agreement holders on commercial fishing operations to permit accumulation of capital for use in approved commercial fishing vessel acquisition or reconstruction projects.

Contact: National Oceanic and Atmospheric Administration, National Marine Fisheries Service, Department of Commerce, Financial Services Division, F/TWI, 1825 Connecticut Avenue NW, Washington, DC 20235. Phone (202) 427-2393.

9. IF YOUR FISHING BOAT OR GEAR IS DESTROYED

If your fishing boat is destroyed by a foreign vessel or if your fishing gear is damaged by an oil-related activity, the government may make direct payments to you.

a. Boat Destruction

In 1988, approximately 135 claims for fishing boat destruction totaling $1 million were paid. The claims ranged from $600 to $150,000.

The applicant must be a U.S. commercial fisherman and a U.S. citizen. The incident must have occurred within the U.S. Fishery Conservation zone or in an area where the United States has exclusive management authority. You need to keep affidavits, receipts, log books, and inventories to show you're a fisherman and owned the property for which compensation is claimed.

b. Gear Loss

If you lost gear because of an oil- or gas-related activity in any area of the outer Continental Shelf, the government will pay for the gear plus 50% of the resulting economic loss.

In 1988 approximately 115 claims for gear damage, ranging from $500 to $25,000, were paid, totaling $700,000.

There are no restrictions on the use of these funds.

You must present financial statements, receipts, log books, and affidavits to establish you are a fisherman and owned the equipment for which compensation is claimed.

Contact: Financial Services Division, Attn: National Marine Fisheries Service, Department of Commerce, 1825 Connecticut Ave. NW, Washington, DC 20235. Phone (202) 427-2390.

10. IF YOUR FISHING BOAT IS SEIZED

The **Department of State** will reimburse you if your fishing boat is seized by a foreign country on the high seas.

In addition, if the seizure occurs in waters claimed by the foreign country as territorial, but the claim is not recognized by the United States, the State Department will still pay.

Pre-registration and payment of a premium fee are necessary.

Losses payable are limited to the market value of the fish before seizure, market value of the boat and gear, and 50% of the gross income lost.

In 1988, 45 claims totaling $1.8 million were paid. Whether or not you pre-register, the government will reimburse you for fines paid to a foreign government to secure the release of your boat.

Contact: Office of Fisheries Affairs, Bureau of Oceans and International Environmental and Scientific Affairs, Room 5806, Department of State, Washington, DC 20520. Phone Stetson Tinkham at (202) 647-1948.

11. MINORITY LOANS FOR DEPARTMENT OF ENERGY RESEARCH

The minority loan program was established to assist minority business enterprises in participating fully in DOE research, development, demonstration and contract activities. The financial assistance is in the form of direct loans, whereby DOE will provide funds to a minority business borrower from its appropriated funds.

The loans are to assist a minority business borrower in financing up to 75% of costs a borrower incurs in preparing a bid or proposal to attempt to obtain DOE contracts or agreements.

The maximum amount of money that can be borrowed for any one loan is $50,000.

Contact: Minority Economic Impact Office, Department of Energy, 1000 Independence Avenue SW, Room 5B-110, Washington, DC 20585. Phone (202) 586-1594.

12. FINANCING OF ARCHITECTURAL AND ENGINEERING OVERSEAS PROJECTS.

The **Export-Import Bank (Eximbank)** provides financing to help U.S. architectural and engineering firms win foreign contracts for project-related feasibility studies and pre-construction engineering services. Under the program, **Eximbank**, the U.S. Government agency charged with facilitating financing for U.S. exports, offers medium-term loans directly to the foreign purchasers of those services, and guarantees private financing for a portion of the local costs of the project.

To qualify for the program, the contract must involve a project with the potential to generate additional U.S. exports worth $10 million or twice the amount of the initial contract, whichever is greater.

Contact: Export-Import Bank of the United States, 811 Vermont Avenue NW, Washington, DC 20571. Phone toll-free (800) 424-5201; firms in Alaska, Hawaii and Washington D.C. should call (202) 566-8860.

13. INSURANCE ON CREDIT TO FOREIGNERS

American companies often find that extending credit to foreign buyers is essential to expand or win business. But distance, unfamiliar legal procedures and unforeseen political or economic events make credit sales to foreign buyers riskier than similar sales to domestic customers.

Eximbank's Policies, offered through its agent, the **Foreign Credit Insurance Association** (FCIA), makes it easier for companies, even those with little or no exporting experience, to get credit risk protection for their export credit sales.

Four policies are offered: **New-to-Export Policy, Umbrella Insurance Policy, Short-Term Multi-Buyer Policy**, and **Bank-to-Bank Letter of Credit Policy**. Products and services include consumables, raw materials, spare parts, agricultural commodities, capital goods, consumer durables and services.

The **Umbrella Policy** enables state and local government agencies, banks, export trading companies, freight forwarders and other financial and professional organizations to become administrators of short-term credit risk insurance covering the export sales of numerous exporters. These administrators assume responsibility for collecting premiums, reporting shipments, filling out forms and processing claims on behalf of the exporters insured under their **Umbrella Policy**.

This policy gives new exporters greater access to foreign credit risk protection and lessens their paperwork burdens. It also helps exporters get financing because the policy proceeds are assignable to any financial institution as collateral on a hold harmless basis. Administrators of Umbrella Policies benefit as well. The Umbrella Policy enables them to offer an important service to their small- and medium-size business customers.

The **New-to-Export Policy** assists companies which are just beginning to export or have an annual export sales volume of less than $750,000. The **Short-Term Multi-Buyer Policy** is available for any exporter. The **Bank-to-Bank Letter of Credit Policy** is available to any bank financing export sales on an irrevocable letter of credit basis.

Contact: Export-Import Bank of the United States, 811 Vermont Avenue, N.W., Washington, DC 20571. Phone toll-free (800) 424-5201; firms in Alaska, Hawaii and Washington DC should call (202) 566-8860.

14. FIXED RATE LOANS FOR EXPORTS

In addition to the risk that a foreign obligator will not repay an export loan, a commercial bank providing export financing faces the risk that its cost of money will rise before the loan is repaid. For this reason, banks generally prefer to extend floating rate loans. Foreign purchasers, however, are frequently unwilling to accept a fluctuating interest rate risk in addition to the foreign exchange risk they bear on foreign currency loans.

Eximbank's **Medium-Term Intermediary Loan Program** enables commercial lenders to offer fixed rate export loans to finance sales of U.S. companies' products and services. In cases where the business is not small, the exporter must face officially supported subsidized foreign competition.

Interest rates are fixed at the lowest rate permitted under the export credit guidelines followed by members of the **Organization for Economic Cooperation and Development (OECD)**.

The OECD rates are reviewed every six months and adjusted as necessary to reflect changes in prevailing interest rates. This program enables financing institutions unrelated to the exporter to borrow from Eximbank below the rate on the export loan, and is used to support sales of goods and services customarily sold on credit terms of one to five years, such as automobiles, trucks, construction equipment and feasibility studies. For more information ask about **Intermediary Loans**.

Contact: Export-Import Bank of the United States, 811 Vermont Avenue NW, Washington, DC 20571. Phone Larry Luther toll-free at (800) 424-5201; firms in Alaska, Hawaii and Washington DC should call (202) 566-8860.

15. GET A REVOLVING LINE OF CREDIT FOR EXPORTS

The **Export Revolving Line of Credit Loan Program (ERLC)** is designed to help more small businesses export their products and services abroad. Any number of withdrawals and repayments can be made as long as the dollar limit of the line is not exceeded and the repayments are made within the stated maturity period, not to exceed 18 months.

Proceeds can be used only to finance labor and materials needed for manufacturing or wholesaling for export, and to penetrate or develop foreign markets.

Through this program, SBA can guarantee up to 85% of a bank line of credit (up to a maximum of $500,000) to a small business exporter. (On amounts under $155,000 SBA can guarantee up to 90% of the loan.)

Applicants must qualify as small under SBA's size standards and meet the other eligibility criteria for all SBA loans. In addition, an applicant must have been in business (not necessarily in exporting) for at least 12 full months prior to filing an application.

ERLC loans are available only under SBA's **Guaranty Plan**. A prospective applicant should review the export financing needs of the business with their bank. If the bank is unable or unwilling to make the loan directly, the possibilities of a participation with SBA should be explored. The participation of a private lender is necessary in order to consummate an ERLC.

Contact: Export Revolving Line of Credit Loan Program (ERLC), Small Business Administration, 1441 L Street NW, Washington, DC 20416.

16. ANOTHER SOURCE OF EXPORT LOAN GUARANTEES

The **SBA-EXIM Co-Guarantee Program** provides for co-guarantees to small business exporters and export trading companies. The co-guarantees extends to loans in principal amounts ranging from $200,000 to $1 million on a per-borrower basis and covers 85% of the loan amount.

The terms and conditions of co-guarantees, except where otherwise provided, are determined by SBA rules and regulations for **Export Revolving Line of Credit** (ERLC) loans.

Proceeds may be used only to finance labor and materials needed for manufacturing or wholesaling for export, and to penetrate or develop foreign markets.

Contact: Small Business Administration, 1441 L Street NW, Washington, DC 20416.

17. YET ANOTHER SOURCE OF LOAN GUARANTEES; THIS ONE HAS INSURANCE FOR EXPORTERS TOO

The Overseas Private Investment Corporation (a government agency) offers the **Contractors and Exporters Program** to improve the competitive position of American contractors and exporters seeking to do business in the developing nations. OPIC offers specialized insurance and financing services.

Many developing countries require foreign firms to post bid, performance or advance payment guarantees in the form of standby letters of credit when bidding on or performing overseas contracts. OPIC's political risk insurance for contractors and exporters protects against the arbitrary or unfair drawing of such letters of credit.

In addition, contractors and exporters may obtain insurance against the risks of currency inconvertibility; confiscation of tangible assets and bank accounts; war, revolution, insurrection and civil strife; and losses sustained when a government owner fails to settle a dispute in accordance with the provisions of the underlying contract.

OPIC also offers a special loan guaranty program for small business contractors to assist with their credit needs. This plan provides an OPIC guaranty of up to 75% of a stand-by letter of credit that is issued to a financial institution on behalf of a small-business contractor.

Contact: Overseas Private Investment Corporation, 1615 M Street NW, Washington, DC 20527. Phone toll-free (800) 424-6742; for businesses within Washington, DC call (202) 457-7010.

18. WORKING CAPITAL GUARANTEES FOR EXPORTERS

Exporting is an important opportunity for many American companies. Sometimes, however, small- and medium-size businesses have trouble obtaining the working capital they need to produce and market goods and services for sale abroad.

Despite their credit worthiness, these potential exporters find commercial banks and other lenders reluctant to offer them working capital financing. Some companies have already reached the borrowing limits set for them by their banks.

Others do not have the type or amount of collateral their banks require. That's why the **Export-Import Bank** of the United States developed the program. **Eximbank** does not lend to exporters directly. Instead, it encourages commercial banks and other lenders to make working capital loans by guaranteeing that, in the event of default by the exporter, Eximbank will repay most of the loan.

For more information ask about the Working Capital Guarantee Program.

Contact: Export-Import Bank of the United States, 811 Vermont Avenue NW, Washington, DC 20571. Phone toll-free (800) 424-5201; firms in Alaska, Hawaii and Washington D.C. should call (202) 566-8860.

19. MONEY AND INSURANCE FOR INVESTING IN OVERSEAS VENTURES

American investors planning to share significantly in the equity and management of an oversea venture can often utilize OPIC's finance programs for medium- to long-term financing.

To obtain OPIC financing, the venture must be commercially and financially sound, within the demonstrated competence of the proposed management, and sponsored by an investor having a proven record of success in the same or closely related business.

OPIC's financing commitment of a new venture may extend to, but not exceed, 50% of the total project cost. A larger participation may be considered for an expansion of a successful, existing enterprise.

Currently, OPIC provides financing to investors through two major programs. Direct loans, which are available only for ventures sponsored by, or significantly involving, U.S. small businesses or cooperatives, and Loan guarantees, which are available to all businesses regardless of size.

OPIC will issue a guaranty under which funding can be obtained from a variety of U.S. financial institutions. The guaranty covers both commercial and political risks.

While private investors generally have the capability to assess the commercial aspects of doing business overseas, they may be hesitant to undertake long-term investments abroad, given the political uncertainties of many developing nations. To alleviate these uncertainties, OPIC insures U.S. investments against three major types of political risks.

Inconvertibility coverage protects an investor against the inability to convert into U.S. dollars the local currency received as profits, earnings, or return of capital on an investment. OPIC's inconvertibility coverage also protects against adverse discriminatory exchange rates.

Expropriation protects the investor not only against classic nationalization of enterprises or the taking of property, but also a variety of situations which might be described as 'creeping expropriation.'

Coverage also is provided against political violence for loss due to bellicose actions (war, revolution, insurrection) and politically motivated civil strife.

Contact: Overseas Private Investment Corporation, 1615 M Street NW, Washington, DC 20527. Phone toll-free (800) 424-6742; for businesses in Washington, DC, call (202)457-7010.

20. LOANS FOR THE HANDICAPPED AND FOR VETERANS

Handicapped people and Vietnam and disabled vets unable to obtain financing in the private credit marketplace may be eligible, first, for a guaranteed/insured loan or, alternatively, for a direct loan if no bank will participate in a guaranteed loan. These loans may be used to construct, expand, or convert facilities; to purchase building equipment or materials; or to provide working capital.

The borrower must meet the SBA's definition of a small business. The applicant must be of good character; show an ability to operate a business successfully; have a significant stake in the business; and show that the business can operate on a sound financial basis.

The applicant must be prepared to provide a statement of personal history, personal financial statements, company financial statements, and summary of collateral. The loan must be of such sound value or so secured as to provide reasonable assurance of repayment.

Applications are generally filed in the SBA field office serving the territory where the applicant's business is located. Approval takes thirty to sixty days from the date of the application acceptance, depending on the type of loan. The applicant is notified by an authorization letter from the district SBA office or participating bank.

Contact: The Business Loan Office, Small Business Administration, Room 804, 1441 L Street NW, Washington, DC 20416.

21. ASSISTANCE IN OBTAINING CAPITAL FOR SMALL BUSINESS INNOVATIVE RESEARCH

A system is available to identify potential sources of capital that may help SBIR awardees commercialize their research and development activities. This system is a free service that provides a list of potential investors such as venture capitalists, corporations, and state government programs.

The database is searchable by technology and industry areas, thereby allowing the office to identify the sources of capital most likely to be interested in a particular company.

This system was also designed to assist SBIR awardees seeking Phase II awards which require that special consideration be given to proposals demonstrating Phase III non-Federal capital commitments.

Contact: Innovation, Research, and Technology Office, Small Business Administration, 1441 L Street NW, Room 500, Washington, DC 20416. Phone (202) 653-6458.

22. GRANTS FOR BROADCASTING STATIONS

The **Public Telecommunications Facilities Program** provides grants to assist in the planning and construction of public telecommunications facilities. Special emphasis is placed on extending public broadcasting signals to currently unserved areas. Construction grants are awarded as matching grants up to 75% of the total cost. Planning grants are awarded up to 100% of the funds necessary for planning a project.

Special consideration is given to women and minorities.

Contact: Public Telecommunications Facilities Program, National Telecommunications and Information Administration, U.S. Department of Commerce, Washington, DC 20230. Phone Dennis Connors at (202) 377-5802.

23. MONEY FOR POLLUTION CONTROL

Businesses may be eligible for pollution control financing if they are unable to obtain private financing on terms or at rates comparable to businesses which do not fit the SBA definition of a small business.

Loan proceeds may be used for aspects of constructing and placing into operation any eligible facility which the SBA determines is likely to prevent, reduce, abate, or control noise, air, or water pollution.

SBA has several options for the kinds of financing instruments that can be used. Lenders can also generate funds for the loans by using marketable securities such as taxable bonds and debentures within authorized loan limits. The principal is not to exceed $5 million.

Contact: Small Business Administration, Pollution Control Financing Staff, 1441 L Street NW, Washington, DC 20416. Phone (202) 653-2548.

24. EQUITY LOANS

Equity investments and long-term loans are available from small business investment companies (SBICs) and section 301(d) small business investment companies (301(d)s) which are privately owned firms licensed by the SBA and partly funded by the Federal government.

Loans must be of at least five years maturity and interest rates, which are subject to negotiation, cannot exceed 15%. SBICs and 301(d)s generally emphasize income-generating investments, such as convertible debentures and straight long-term debt. They tend to be most active in providing growth capital to established businesses, and are active in financing high-technology, start-up enterprises.

The applicant should prepare a business plan that describes its operations, financial condition, and financing requirements — detailing information on products, new product lines, patent positions, market and competitive data, sales and distribution, key personnel, and other pertinent factors.

Your nearest SCORE office can be of help in preparing the proper business plan. See the section on SCORE, the Service Corp of Retired Executives. Note that Section 301(d) SBICs finance only socially or economically disadvantaged small business.

Contact: Small Business Administration, Office of SBIC Operations, Room 810, 1441 L Street NW, Washington, DC 20416. Phone (202) 653-6584.

25. SAVE MONEY ON TAXES, BECOME A FOREIGN SALES CORPORATION

A **Foreign Sales Corporation** (FSC) is a corporation at up is a qualifying foreign nation or U.S. possession that obtains an exemption on corporate taxes on a portion of the profits earned on exports or services. Usually 15% of the profits are tax-free.

There are "regular" FSCs and Small FSCs; Small FSCs' rules are easier to cope with.

To get a brochure on the rules and some applications call Helen Burroughs at (202) 377-3277 or write the Office of Trade Finance, U.S. Department of Commerce, International Trade Administration, Washington, DC 20230.

26. STARTING A FEDERAL CREDIT UNION

The **National Credit Union Administration** will explain how to get started, help prepare the charter application, assist in start-up operations and provide depositor insurance.

For established credit unions in low-income communities, they also have direct loans.

The guidelines for eligibility are that you can start a credit union if you have an association with at least 300 members, have an employee group of 200 or more, or live in a rural community with 500 or more families. In 1987, 315 new federal credit union charters were granted.

For more information ask for the Credit Union Information Package. Contact: National Credit Union Administration, 1776 G. St. NW, Washington, DC 20456. Phone (202) 682-1900. For information on loans phone Mr. Floyd Lancaster at (202) 682-9780.

27. ECONOMIC INJURY DISASTER LOANS

The **Disaster Assistance Division** of the Small Business Administration can help if your business concern suffers economic injury as a result of natural disasters. If the business was within the disaster area, see the next entry, Physical Disaster Loans.

In 1987, 585 of these loans were made for $43 million. The terms are up to thirty years for repayment with a $500,000 limit.

The funds are for paying current liabilities which the small concern could have paid if the disaster had not occurred. Working capital for a limited period can be provided to continue operations until conditions return to normal.

For more information request the pamphlet *Economic Injury Disaster Loans for Small Business.*

Contact: Disaster Assistance Division, Small Business Administration, 1441 L Street NW, Washington, DC 20416. Phone (202) 653-6879.

28. PHYSICAL DISASTER LOANS

The **Disaster Assistance Division** of the Small Business Administration can help if your business is physically damaged by a natural disaster such as a hurricane, flood, or tornado. If your business is not physically damaged, but suffers economically, see the preceding section, Economic Injury Disaster Loans.

In 1988, 22,000 loans were made for $350 million. In general the terms are for thirty years, with a limit of $500,000, although if high unemployment will result, the amount can be higher. The SBA will establish an on-site office to help with processing and disbursement.

For more information request the pamphlet *Physical Disaster Loans.*

Contact: Disaster Assistance Division, Small Business Administration, 1441 L Street NW, Washington, DC 20416. Phone (202) 653-6879.

29. IF YOU NEED A PERFORMANCE BOND AND CAN'T GET ONE

Small contractors may find, for whatever reasons, bonding unavailable to them. If so, the Small Business Administration is authorized to guarantee to a qualified surety up to 90% of losses incurred under bid, payment, or performance bonds issued to contractors on contracts valued up to $1 million. The contracts may be for construction, supplies, or services provided by either a prime or subcontractor.

In 1987, 10,382 contractors were helped. The loan guarantees for 1989 are expected to be over $1 billion dollars.

Contact: Office of Surety Guarantees, Small Business Administration, 4040 N. Fairfax Dr., Arlington, VA 22203. Phone James W. Parker at (703) 235-2900.

30. LOCAL DEVELOPMENT COMPANY LOANS

Groups of local citizens whose aim is to improve the economy in their area can get a **Certified Development Company Loan.** Loan proceeds may be used to finance residential or commercial construction or rehabilitation of property for sale.

In 1987, 1,546 loans were made. The estimated total money available for 1989 is $415 million.

Contact your local small business administration office.

31. START A SMALL AIRLINE

If you'd like to provide air services to small towns, the Department of Transportation may be able to help. They subsidize service to approximately 150 communities that would not otherwise have air access. The payments cover costs and return needs. The annual payments range from $90,000 to $400,000 per destination. Approximately twenty-eight million dollars were paid in 1988.

Contact: Director, Office of Aviation Analysis, P-50, Department of Transportation, 400 Seventh St. SW, Washington, DC 20590. Phone (202) 366-1030.

32. FLOOD INSURANCE

The Federal Insurance Administration enables persons and small businesses to purchase insurance against losses from physical damage to buildings and their contents. The premium rate is generally lower than a normal actuarial rate, reflecting a subsidy by the Federal Government. Maximum coverage is $250,000 for small business structures and $300,000 for the contents.

They have a large number of booklets available, which explains the program, design guidelines for floor damage reduction, how to understand flood insurance rate maps, etc.

Contact: Federal Insurance Administration, FEMA, Washington, DC 20472. Phone David Cobb at (202) 646-2774.

33. WRESTLING WITH TAX MATTERS

The *Your Business Tax Kit*, publication 454, was developed for presentation to operators of new businesses as they are formed. Its purpose is to encourage more effective voluntary compliance by helping new business persons become fully aware of their responsibilities for filing all the Federal tax returns for which they may be liable and for paying the taxes due.

The kit is an envelope designed to hold forms and instructions for preparing most business tax returns.

Kits may either be picked up at an IRS office or will be mailed to the taxpayer upon request.

The IRS also annually publishes a *Tax Guide for Small Business*, Publication 334, which explains Federal tax programs for sole proprietors, partners, partnerships, and corporations.

Small Business Tax Workshops are conducted regularly throughout the country. For more information or to request a publication, call toll-free 1-800-424-1040.

34. EMERGENCY LOANS FOR FARMERS
AND RANCHERS

The **Farmers Home Administration** has loans to assist family farmers, ranchers and agriculture operators to cover losses suffered from major disasters. Loans may be used to repair, restore, or replace damaged property and supplies and, under some circumstances, to refinance debts.

The maximum loan is $500,000; the interest rate is 4.5 percent. In 1987, 2,548 loans totaling $113 million were made.

Contact: Farmers Home Administration, Department of Agriculture, Washington, DC 20250. Phone (202) 382-1632.

35. LOANS FOR NON-PROFIT CORPORATIONS

The **Farmers Home Administration** has loans, loan guarantees, and grants to rural development and finance corporations that improve business, industry and employment in rural areas through the stimulation of private investment and foundation contributions.

The non-profit corporation may serve profit or non-profit businesses but they must be local. The corporation must be authorized to do business in at least three states.

For more information, contact: Administrator, Farmers Home Administration, Department of Agriculture, Washington, DC 20250. Phone (202) 447-7967.

36. MONEY FOR NOT GROWING STUFF

If your green thumb has turned yellow, this is for you. For not growing cotton, corn, sorghum, barley, oats, wheat, or rice, the Department of Agriculture will reward you. What's the catch? You must do this by reducing the amount you usually produce.

Contact: Commodity Analysis Division, Agricultural Stabilization and Conservation Service, P. O. Box 2415, U. S. Department of Agriculture, Washington, DC 20013. Phone (202) 447-6734.

37. SMALL FOREST PROJECTS

If you own 1,000 acres or less of forest land capable of producing industrial wood crops, the Forestry Incentives Program may be of interest. The government will share up to 65 percent of the cost of tree planting, timber stand improvement, and site preparation. In 1989 approximately eight million dollars in cost-share assistance will be provided.

Contact: Conservation and Environmental Protection Division, Department of Agriculture, P. O. Box 2415, Washington, DC 20013. Phone (202) 447-6221.

38. MONEY FOR SHIPS

The Department of Transportation Maritime Administration will provide loan guarantees to promote the construction of ships for foreign and domestic commerce.

The vessels must be designed for research or for commercial use in coastal or intercoastal trade, on the Great

Lakes, on bays, rivers, lakes, etc., of the U.S., in foreign trade, or as floating drydocks. Any ship not less than five net tons (other than a towboat, barge, scow, lighter, canal boat or tank vessel of less than 25 gross tons) is eligible.

The ship owner must provide 25% of the total cost. These guarantees have been used to build large ships such as tankers, ocean-going liners, dredges, jack-up drilling rigs, and container ships. Numerous smaller ships including ocean-going and inland tugs and barges have also been funded.

Contact: Associate Administrator for Maritime Aids, Maritime Administration, Department of Transportation, Washington, DC 20590. Phone (202) 366-0364.

39. MORTGAGE INSURANCE

If you rent housing to low or middle income, the elderly, in urban renewal areas, or are a credit risk because of low income, the Department of Housing and Urban Development may be able to help by providing mortgage insurance.

Contact: Insurance Division, Office of Insured Multi-family Housing Development, Department of Housing and Urband Development, Washington, DC 20410. Phone (202) 755-6223.

40. GRANTS FOR DESIGNING PEOPLE

Grants for architecture, landscaping, fashion design, interior decorating, and urban design are available from the National Endowment of the Arts.

Examples of projects that have been funded are: an urban design plan for the revitalization of a city waterfront district, a design competition for a museum of fine arts, adaptive reuse of unused school buildings, and the potential uses for vacant and derelict land in American cities.

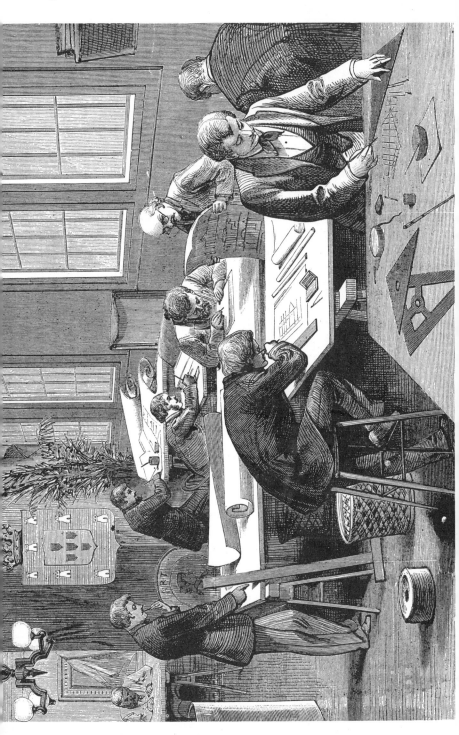

In 1989 over 4 million dollars will be awarded. Ask for the booklets *National Endowment for the Arts*, *Guide to Programs* and *Design Arts Guidelines*.

Contact: Director, Design Arts Program, National Endowment for the Arts, 1100 Pennsylvania Ave. NW, Washington, DC 20506. Phone (202) 682-5437.

41. WHAT TO DO IF THE GOVERNMENT WON'T GIVE YOU A LOAN

Don't be disheartened; there are a number of options open to you. One of them may be even better than a government loan.

a. If you're sure money is the answer to your problem, get a copy of *Free Money for Small Businesses and Entrepreneurs* described in Appendix II.

Free Money has over 300 sources, including foundations, state and local governments, private funds, and others.

After picking the applicable foundations for your situation, write or call them for a copy of their guidelines.

Grant applications take time to fill out, but the same material for one can be used for most of them. *Free Money* contains some sample grant proposals.

Foundations will invest in enterprises that most others would consider too speculative, so they're especially invaluable for start-ups.

There are dozens of categories of businesses to check; for instance, some of the specialized foundations are oriented toward ecology, civil rights, Jewish immigrants, Russian immigrants, and historical restorations. Some are to be used only within a particular state or county. Many address a certain area of business, e.g., financial businesses, manufacturing. Some are oriented toward the generation of jobs.

b. A different approach to owning a successful business avoids loans from institutions. A brief outline of the technique goes as follows:

- **Most new businesses fail,** so avoid this obstacle by owning a proven successful business.
- **All businesses are for sale.** The next time you go into a business that looks prosperous and interesting to you, ask who the owner is. If he's on the premises, go into his office; if not, phone him from the nearest phone booth. Ask him, "Have you ever thought about selling this business?" The answer is always yes. Tell him you're interested. Plan on seeing him a number of times for informal discussions.
- **The owner will ask you, "How much have you got to put down?"** Say that the amount put down depends on the financial status of the company, but you will need some owner financing. Usually they'll say that if you will put twenty to thirty percent down, they'll provide financing. Be sure to ask for twenty- to thirrty-year financing. Don't worry about not having the down payment in hand.
- **Make sure the company makes a good profit;** it is easier to buy a company that has $200,000 to $300,000 a year profit than it is to buy one that makes $10,000 a year profit. Besides going through the books ask their suppliers. Suppliers know which businesses are profitable.
- **Is the company run by a manager?** Has he been there more than five years? If so, ask him if he'll stay if you buy the business.
- **Who are the suppliers?** Contact them and ask them what they think about the prospective business. If they are enthused, tell them you want to buy the business and will need some "working capital" (*this is your down payment but never call it that*). You may need to grant him exclusive rights to supply you, or other similar concessions. There is a large variety of interbusiness financial agreements. Usually one will fit your purposes. *This is the largest source of business loans in the U.S. today.*

That's the approach in a nutshell. There are many variations on the theme.

There are a number of seminars that teach this basic method. Watch for one in your area.

Chapter 8

INTERNATIONAL TRADE

1. EXPORT COUNSELING AND FINANCIAL ASSISTANCE

The **Office of International Trade** facilitates financial assistance and other appropriate management and technical assistance to small business concerns that have the potential to become successful exporters. The program provides basic export counseling and training which includes:

(1) one-on-one counseling by SCORE/ACE volunteers with significant international trade expertise;

(2) access to university research and counseling;

(3) assistance from professional international trade management consulting firms;

(4) referral to other public or private sector expertise;

(5) initial consultation with an international trade attorney of the Federal Bar Association;

(6) business management training;

(7) international trade and export marketing publications.

Contact: Office of International Trade, Small Business Administration, 1441 L Street NW, Washington, DC 20416. Phone (202) 653-7794.

2. EXPORT SEMINARS

The **Bureau of Export Administration's** seminar staff teaches exporters about the national security requirements for international sales. U.S. exporters and foreign importers of American products around the world increase their knowledge and understanding of U.S. Export Regulations by attending classroom instruction offered by the export seminar staff. The Export Administration Regulations Course is a professional seminar featuring two or three days of classroom training on export controls and licensing procedures.

Seminars are held in major cities throughout the United States and in foreign countries. Both introductory and advanced courses on the Export Administration Regulations are offered. Completing the introductory course is a prerequisite for receiving advanced instruction.

The seminars assist a business in understanding the requirements for compliance with U.S. export laws and procedures, to improve its ability to use and understand federal export regulations, to prepare better license applications and other documentation, to find out how a company can avoid the costly fines and time-consuming seizures that result from violation of export laws, and to discover ways to increase productivity, ease license application efforts, and lower costs of doing business abroad.

These seminars have proven valuable to manufacturers, carriers, shipping agents, freight forwarders, international sales and marketing specialists, contracts administrators, materials and traffic managers, customer service representatives, buyers, accountants, attorneys, freight forwarders, technical supervisors, order processors, and export licensing coordinators.

Contact: Bureau of Export Administration, Department of Commerce, 14th & Constitution Avenue, NW, HCHB

Room 1608, Washington, DC 20230. Phone (202) 377-8731.

3. EXPORT MANAGEMENT AND MARKETING HELP FOR SMALLER BUSINESSES

The **Agency for International Development** (AID) implements the U.S. Foreign Economic Assistance Program in more than 60 countries throughout Africa, Asia/Near East, and Latin America and the Caribbean. The office offers counseling services and marketing assistance to U.S. firms wishing to export goods through AID-financed commodities programs.

Businesses are counseled on marketing approaches, interpreting and adhering to AID and other Federal export regulations, and completing required AID documentations. Also, OSBDU/MRC publishes (through Procurement Information Bulletins and Small Business Circulars) notices of intended procurement of AID-financed commodities by foreign purchasers.

These notices are available free of charge by completing a mailing list application available from the office. Also available for those on the mailing list are Importer Lists for selected AID-recipient countries and Small Business Memos which contain trade, policy, and procedural information of general value.

The agency participates in two procurement set-aside programs administered by the Small Business Administration (SBA) — the small business set-aside program and the 8(a) set-aside program. Contracts that are not set-aside through these programs are advertised for open competition in the *Commerce Business Daily* (CBD), a publication of the U.S. Department of Commerce.

The office maintains the AID Consultant Registry Information System (ACRIS), an automated database identifying capabilities of companies, organizations, and individual consultants/experts wishing to participate in AID-financed projects.

Contact: Agency for International Development, Office of Small and Disadvantaged Business Utilization (OSDBU), Department of State, OSBDU/MRC, Washington, DC 20523. Phone (703) 875-1590.

4. HOW THE GOVERNMENT WILL PROMOTE YOUR PRODUCT OVERSEAS

The International Trade Administration's **Export Promotion Services** will assist exporters through a variety of programs and services that analyze foreign markets, locate buyers and representatives overseas, and promote products and services. In addition, they offer export counseling services for all aspects of the export process. International trade experts are located worldwide in 66 U.S. cities and 127 overseas cities.

Trade Fairs are shop windows in which thousands of firms from many countries display their wares. These fairs are international marketplaces in which buyers and sellers can meet conveniently.

A **Trade Fair Certification Program** advises and assists sponsors of these fairs in promoting the events; gives the fairs official Department of Commerce recognition; and counsels exhibitors. In addition, official U.S. participation is sponsored in key international trade fairs in all parts of the world.

Three types of trade missions have been developed to help U.S. exporters penetrate overseas markets. **Specialized Trade Missions** bring groups of U.S. business people into direct contact with potential foreign buyers, agents, and distributors.

Seminar Missions promote sales of sophisticated products and technology in markets where sales can be achieved more effectively by presenting technical seminars or concentrating on concepts and systems. They feature one- and two-day presentations by a team of U.S. industry representatives who conduct discussions on the technology of their industry.

Industry-Organized Government-Approved (IOGA) Trade Missions are organized by trade associations, chambers of commerce, state development agencies, and similar groups with the advice and support of the agency.

In addition to product exhibitions, the overseas Export Development Office facilities are available to trade associations and to individual firms or their agents for Business-Sponsored Promotions (BSPs). BSPs may include sales meetings, conferences, or seminars. Finally, Catalog Exhibitions and Video/Catalog Exhibitions are low-cost, flexible kinds of exhibitions that can provide U.S. industry with an effective technique to give products exposure overseas, test the salability of the products, develop sales leads, and identify potential buyers, agents, or distributors.

Both are held at U.S. Embassies or Consulates or in conjunction with trade shows. These two kinds of exhibitions are especially useful in promoting U.S. exports in remote and small markets of the world where major equipment exhibitions are not feasible.

Contact: International Trade Administration, United States and Foreign Commercial Service, Department of Commerce, Export Promotion Services, 14th & Constitution Avenue NW, Room 2116H, Washington, DC 20230. Phone (202) 377-4231.

5. APPLYING FOR AN EXPORT LICENSE

The **Bureau of Export Administration** has several services to assist in the licensing process. This office is the bureau's licensing 'customer service unit' staffed with licensing information experts. It helps solve or answer most exporters' questions about 'How to apply for an export license.' By telephone or mail, these experts can help you prepare license applications and guide you through export regulations.

In developing an export strategy, companies need to review the U.S. export laws as they relate to a planned export. For reasons of national security, export of certain technologies is controlled through two types of export licenses: general and validated.

This office should be called when you have a specific question about export regulations or current policy, need license information on overseas trade fairs, have an emergency license request that may need special handling, or want to find out your licensing case number.

ELIAN (Electronic License Application Information Network) allows online computer acceptance of export license applications for all free world destinations. ELAIN offers U.S. exporters a fast and convenient way to submit or receive license applications. After receiving applications, the office processes, reviews, and issues the license electronically. Applications may cover all commodities except super-computers.

First, exporters apply for authorization to submit applications electronically by writing to the address above to the attention of ELAIN. The exporter should provide the name and address of the applicant company, a phone number, and the name of the contact person.

The **Office of Exporting Licensing** will provide information on how to obtain company identifications numbers and personal identification numbers to individuals approved by the office and the exporting company to submit license applications. The exporter will also receive instructions on how to contact the CompuServe computer network to obtain detailed filing instructions.

Once exporters have the necessary authorization to begin submitting license applications electronically to ELAIN, they will be able to enter license related information into their own personal computers and send it over telephone lines via CompuServe to the Commerce Department. Licensing decisions will be electronically conveyed back to exporters, again via the CompuServe network.

They'll help you get export licensing publications and forms, the most important of which is *Export Administration Regulations*. Other publications available include the

Index to Commodity Control List and *Export Control of Technical Data.*

Since the Bureau of Export Administration receives between 500 and 600 applications every working day, it is important for a business to obtain these information publications early in the marketing stage so that it fully understands the export licensing program.

To subscribe to the *Export Administration Regulations* contact the Superintendent of Documents, U.S. GPO, Washington, DC 20402. Phone (202) 783-3238. Reference subscription number 903-012-00000-5.

Exporters may obtain forms required by the bureau by calling the Exporter Assistance staff at (202) 377-8731 or writing Bureau of Export Administration, Department of Commerce, P.O. Box 273, Washington, DC 20044. ATTN: FORMS.

STELA (System for Tracking Export License Applications) is a computer-generated voice unit that interfaces with the Department of Commerce ECASS (Export Control Automated Support System) database. It provides accurate and timely information on the status of license applications.

STELA tells an exporter exactly where an application is in the system and for how long it has been there. It can also give an exporter authority to ship his or her goods for those applications approved without conditions. Exporters still receive a hard copy of the license by mail, but an exporter can ship with STELA's approval before receiving it.

Exporters, with a touch-tone phone, can call STELA at (202) 377-2752, it will answer "Hello, I'm STELA, the Department of Commerce export license system. Please enter your license application number or hang up." Using the pushbuttons on the phone, enter the license application number. Following the entry, in synthesized voice response, STELA gives the status of the case. If you need to talk to a person about STELA, call (202) 377-2572.

STELA can also handle questions about the amendment applications. After announcing the status of one case, STELA prompts the caller to enter another case number or hang up. STELA is in operation weekdays from

7:15 a.m. to 11:15 p.m. EST and on Saturdays from 8:00 a.m. to 4:00 p.m. The database is updated each night, so an application's status should be checked only once a day.

Contact: Bureau of Export Administration, Department of Commerce, 14th & Constitution Avenue NW, HCHB Room 1099D, Washington, DC 20230. Phone (202) 377-4811 in Washington, DC or (714) 660-0144 in Newport CA.

6. HOW TO FIND NEW OPPORTUNITIES IN FOREIGN MARKETS

Competition in the world market is becoming ever more challenging and foreign governments have increased support for their exporters. The Export Trading Company Act of 1982 offers U.S. business new opportunities to compete in foreign markets. The goal of this legislation is to encourage the development of American Export Trading Companies (ETC), particularly for the benefit of small and medium-sized companies.

This office promotes and encourages the formation of ETCs, counsels firms interested in exporting, provides a contact facilitation service between U.S. producers and firms providing export trade services, administers the Title III antitrust Certificate of Review Program, and conducts ETC conferences.

Contact: The Export Trading Company Affairs Office, International Trade Administration, Trade Development, Department of Commerce, 14th & Constitution Avenue NW, Washington, DC 20230. Phone (202) 377-5131.

7. IDENTIFYING AND EVALUATING OVERSEAS MARKETS

The new **Commercial Information Management System (CIMS)** electronically links all the economic and marketing information of ITA trade specialists and offices worldwide, allowing vital business data to be delivered on a timely basis.

Custom tailored market research information packages are available on foreign business and economic climate, import regulations, tariff and non-tariff barriers, domestic and foreign competition, individual competitor firms and competitive factors, distribution practices, how products are promoted in the market, policies, and product standards; and end users.

In addition, CIMS can provide information on foreign agents, distributors, importers, manufacturers, retailers, government purchasing officials, and end users interested in your product or service type. CIMS can provide names, contacts, telex and telephone numbers, cable addresses, product or service specialties, year established, number of employees and relative size, all tailored to the specifications you supply.

Contact: CIMS Market Research, International Trade Administration, United States and Foreign Commercial Service, Department of Commerce, 14th & Constitution Avenue NW, Washington, DC 20230.

8. LISTS OF OVERSEAS CUSTOMERS AND COMPANIES

The Export Information Systems (XIS) **Data Reports** provides lists of the largest markets and competition sources for a company's product.

Available for approximately 1,700 Standard International Trade Classification (SITC) product categories, the **XIS Data Reports** based on United Nations data will provide to the small business owner a list of the 25 largest importing markets for his or her product, the 10 best markets for U.S. exporters of that product, the trends within those markets, and the major sources of foreign competition.

This information will help a business to decide whether or not to export and, if so, which markets to research further, using Department of Commerce market information as well as other, more in-depth marketing services.

Contact: Export Information Systems (XIS), Small Business Administration, 1441 L Street NW, Washington, DC 20416.

9. ADVERTISING TO 100,000 FOREIGN EXECUTIVES, DISTRIBUTORS, AND GOVERNMENT OFFICIALS

Commercial News USA promotes U.S. products and services available for export to more than 100,000 overseas agents, distributors, government officials, and end-users. Additional distribution is made of selected products and services through reprints in local media.

Commercial News USA contains descriptions of 150 to 200 products, services, and trade and technical literature with black and white photographs in each issue. In addition to featuring general new products, all issues highlight individual industries and receive special promotion by U.S. commercial officers overseas at industry trade events.

While much depends on the product being promoted, firms typically average thirty to forty inquiries each and initial sales averaging over $10,000. There is a fee for publishing in the magazine.

Contact: International Trade Administration, United States and Foreign Commercial Service, Department of Commerce, 14th & Constitution Avenue NW, Washington, DC 20230.

10. TRADE LEADS ON OVERSEAS SALES OPPORTUNITIES FOR AGRICULTURAL-RELATED PRODUCTS

The Agricultural Information and Marketing Services (AIMS) **Trade Lead Service** provides continual access to timely sales leads from overseas firms seeking to buy or represent American food and agricultural products. Businesses have a direct pipeline to trade leads gathered by Foreign Agricultural Service (FAS) offices worldwide.

Both new and established American exporters can use trade leads as a fundamental sales tool which brings foreign buyers' purchasing needs directly to them.

Each day, FAS agricultural counselors, attachés, and trade officers around the world locate and develop trade opportunities. They find sales opportunities with foreign companies, government purchasing agencies, brokers, distributors and others, and determine information needed to pursue each trade lead-product specifications such as labeling and packaging, quantities, end uses, delivery deadlines, bid requirements, telex/cable contact points, and mailing addresses. These trade leads are then forwarded to AIMS within hours, and distributed.

Leads are available the same day to U.S. exporters through a number of commercial computerized information networks. Trade leads also can be mailed daily to clients in the United States who have subscribed to a special mail service.

A bulletin is available which includes ALL trade leads processed each week. It is mailed weekly and is targeted toward export agents, trade associations, and companies interested in export opportunities for a wide variety of food and agricultural products.

The bulletin also highlights upcoming trade shows, foreign trade developments, and changes and updates in trade policy. They can also generate various mailing lists of prospective buyers for you.

Contact: Foreign Agricultural Service, Department of Agriculture, Agricultural Information and Marketing Service, 14th & Independence Avenue SW, Room 4649-S, Washington, DC 20250. Phone (202) 447-7103.

11. ALERTING FOREIGN BUYERS

The program is a service offered by the **Agricultural Information and Marketing Services (AIMS)** project. Using high-speed telecommunications links, the AIMS staff in Washington, D.C. forwards company sales announcement of featured products to interested overseas buyers. The AIMS communication network can place information about a product into the hands of foreign buyers who seek U.S. products.

The alert service goes one step beyond product introduction. It transfers actual sales announcements to interested buyers, to generate business.

Each announcement features a product, a short description, an indicator price which is valid through a given date, and information on how to contact the U.S. supplier. These announcements are disseminated to interested importers in the leading value-added export markets for U.S. products.

Contact: Foreign Agricultural Service, Department of Agriculture, Agricultural Information and Marketing Service, 14th & Independence Avenue SW, Room 4649-S, Washington, DC 20250. Phone (202) 447-7103.

12. HELP FOR FOOD EXPORTERS

The **Label Clearance Program** (LCP) was designed to help U.S. food processors and exporters locate foreign markets and sales opportunities for U.S. commodities new to overseas markets.

Although many of these products have long since been tested and accepted by American customers, the products have not been marketed in many foreign countries.

Each participating U.S. firm is provided with information on the foreign countries' requirements for imported foods. Without this information the job of exporting to a foreign market can be costly and time-consuming.

The LCP review can answer such questions as: where must the country of origin appear on the label; in what order must the product ingredients be listed; what is the required language and are bilingual labels or stick-ons acceptable, etc.

The LCP office conducts a screening of each company's label and product information to ensure completeness before it is submitted for overseas evaluation. Once this screening is completed the information is forwarded to LCP review in the targeted country.

The final product specific report prepared by an overseas post contains a brief statement on the product's marketability in the specific overseas country. This objective assessment of the product's ability to compete in the targeted market is provided to assist the U.S. firm in its evaluation of the product's competitiveness.

A new part of the LCP Services is the Country Product Clearance Summary. This report provides the participating company with a concise statement on the taste and eating habits of the country, information on the legal requirements and standards that govern the packaging and labeling of imported foods, and the business customs of the targeted country.

Summary reports for Japan, Mexico, West Germany, Switzerland, and France have been completed.

Contact: The Label Clearance Program, Foreign Agricultural Service, Department of Agriculture, High Value Products Division, 14th & Independence Avenue SW, Room 4649-S, Washington, DC 20250. Phone (202) 447-7103.

13. ADVERTISING YOUR AGRICULTURAL PRODUCTS OVERSEAS

A monthly newsletter, *Contacts for U.S. Agricultural Products*, assists American firms by introducing their food and agricultural products to foreign markets. It is sent to Foreign Agricultural Service counselors, attachés, and trade officers for distribution to prospective foreign buyers.

It is translated into Japanese, Spanish, French, Italian, and Greek and mailed to thousands of buyers worldwide. Brief, 100-word descriptions of products submitted by U.S. firms are published each month.

Contact: Foreign Agricultural Service, Department of Agriculture, Agricultural Information and Marketing Service, 14th & Independence Avenue SW, Room 4649-S, Washington, DC 20250. Phone (202) 447-7103.

14. WHEN AN EXPORT LICENSING EMERGENCY OCCURS

A business may have an emergency when an export license application should receive immediate attention. In justifiable emergencies, generally when the situation is out of the applicant's control, the applicant or his authorized agent should contact this office or the nearest district office to expedite handling of an application.

The validity of a license issued under this special processing procedure expires no later than the last day of the month following the month of issuance. Because a company is expected to use a license issued on an emergency basis immediately, the office of Export Licensing will not extend the validity period of a license.

Contact: Bureau of Export Administration, Office of Export Licensing, Department of Commerce, 14th & Constitution Avenue NW, HCHB Room 1099D, Washington, DC 20230. Phone (202) 377-4811 (Washington, DC) or (714) 660-0144 (Newport Beach, CA).

15. WHEN YOU NEED TECHNICAL ANSWERS FOR PRODUCTS UNDER EXPORT CONTROL

At the request of exporters, advisory options and classification determinations are issued on commodities to be exported from the United States.

The **Technology and Policy Analysis Office** is responsible for establishing export control policy under the authority of the Export Administration Act.

It develops, in association with other U.S. agencies and the international Coordinating Committee (COCOM), export control and decontrol proposals. It analyzes and develops national security, foreign policy, and short supply control programs; revises and develops implementing Export Administration Regulations; and reviews and resolves technical and policy issues related to export applications and appeals of licensing determinations.

Contact: Technology and Policy Analysis Office, Bureau of Export Administration, Department of Commerce, 14th & Constitution Avenue NW, HCHB Room 4069A, Washington, DC 20230. Phone (202) 377-4188.

16. REFERRALS FOR EXPORT RELATED DATA PROCESSING SERVICES

This new service is offered to businesses and others who want to file export documents electronically but do not have access to needed computer hardware and/or software.

The bureau will provide a brochure listing service agencies that have registered with the **Census Bureau** and that can provide one or more of these services: develop or provide computer software, edit raw data; transmit electronic data to the bureau; provide data on computer tape or floppy diskettes, or provide current listings of all commodity classifications.

Registered organizations can supply the services for which they are listed.

Contact: National Clearinghouse for Export Data Processing Services, Bureau of the Census, Automated Export Reporting Office, Department of Commerce, Foreign Trade Division, Room 2114-3, Washington, DC 20233. Phone (301) 763-7774.

17. LOCATING OVERSEAS REPRE-SENTATIVES FOR YOUR FIRM

A unique program provides custom overseas searches for interested and qualified foreign representatives on behalf of a U.S. client.

U.S. commercial officers abroad conduct the search on a single country and prepare a report identifying up to six foreign prospects that have personally examined the U.S. firm's product literature and have expressed interest in representing the firm.

Contact: Agent/Distributor Service (ADS), International Trade Administration, United States and Foreign Commercial Service, Department of Commerce, Washington, DC 20230. Phone (202) 377-3181.

18. OPPORTUNITIES IN THE CARIBBEAN.

The **Caribbean Basin Division** services the U.S. business community by actively translating U.S. trade and investment policies into real business opportunities. Under special mandate of the Caribbean Basin Economic Recovery Act (CBERA) of 1983, the Caribbean Basin Division offers a broad range of services to assist American firms in developing their full trade potential in the Caribbean Basin, as well as introducing them to investment opportunities.

Assistance ranges from initial counseling for companies not yet trading, to special help in obtaining major contracts worth millions of dollars.

The Caribbean Basin country desk officers provide information and counseling on:
Economic and commercial conditions,
Political and social issues,
Trade and investment laws and regulations,
Trade and investment statistics,
Business opportunity leads,
Markets for a given product,
Services available from other U.S. government and commercial agencies.

Contact: Caribbean Basin Division, International Trade Administration, International Economic Policy, Department of Commerce, 14th & Constitution Avenue NW, Room 3314, Washington, DC 20230. Phone (202) 377-2527.

19. TO REACH AN EXPORT SPECIALIST FOR A SPECIFIC COUNTRY

Where should a U.S. exporter go to find out about agent/distributor agreements in Saudi Arabia? About how to recover a business debt resulting from Mexico's foreign exchange crisis? About Canada's investment approval process? About a trade show in Germany? About countertrade with Tanzania? About tariff rates in Paraguay?

The best sources of information on such matters are **country desk officers** who can handle such questions and provide other useful commercial information as well.

These specialists perform a unique service. They look at the needs of the individual U.S. firm wishing to sell in a particular country in the full context of that country's overall economy, trade policies and political situation, and also in the light of U.S. policies toward the country.

Desk officers keep up to date on the economic and commercial conditions in their assigned countries. Each collects information on the country's regulations, tariffs, business practices, economic and political developments including trade data and trends, market size and growth that affect ability to do business. Each keeps tabs on the country's potential as a market for U.S. products and services and for U.S. investment.

Call (202) 377-2000 and ask for the export specialist for the country of interest. To get a complete listing of all countries that have specialists and the name and telephone number, call (202) 377-3265 and ask for the ITA telephone directory.

To write them: Country Export Specialists, International Trade Administration, International Economic Policy, Department of Commerce, 14th & Constitution Avenue NW, Room 3864, Washington, DC 20230.

20. EXPORT MANAGEMENT AND NETWORKING ASSISTANCE NEAR YOU

Businesses help promote and assist in increasing U.S. exports through the International Trade Administration's **District Export Councils**. The councils work to enlist the efforts of the American business community to help government expand export opportunities and increase U.S. exports abroad.

There are 51 councils with 1800 members representing every state and territory of the United States. They have an increased role in the development of U.S. trade policy. Organized work plans are developed by each council to carry out initiatives locally to promote exporting.

The councils have become a vital multiplier in export awareness and promotion and represent a local voice in the establishment of trade policies. Firms interested in contacting their local councils should call this office.

Contact: District Export Councils, International Trade Administration, United States and Foreign Commercial Service, Department of Commerce, 14th & Constitution Avenue NW, Washington, DC 20230. Phone Kevin Mulvey at (202) 377-0332.

21. WHERE TO GET TRADE DATA, COMPETITIVE ASSESSMENTS, AND ANALYSIS DATA

The **Trade Information and Analysis Program** monitors and provides trade data, conducts macro-economic trade research and analysis, assesses U.S. industrial competitiveness, and operates an Office of Trade Finance, which offers counseling on offset/countertrade practices to U.S. exporters.

The program also produces a series of publications, such as *Industrial Outlook*, *Competitive Assessments*, *Trade Performance*, and *U.S. Foreign Trade Highlights*.

Industrial Outlook, published annually, features assessments and forecasts of business conditions for more than 350 industries. It is available at any Government Printing Office for $24.

Competitive Assessments are periodic reports which assess the medium- and long-range competitiveness of specific U.S. industries in international trade.

Some recent titles include *Cement*, *Automobile*, *Materials Handling Equipment*, *Sporting Goods*, *Cellular Radio Equipment*, *International Construction*, *Computer Systems*, *Civil Helicopters*, and *Fiber Optics*. These are available at any Government Printing Office at a cost of between $3 and $7.

The Trade Performance series, published annually, provides a detailed analytical look at the U.S. trade performance and positions.

The *U.S. Foreign Trade Highlights*, published annually, details trade data trends in U.S. foreign trade in selected regions and with major trading partners. The current issue is available at any Government Printing Office.

Contact a Government Printing Office or International Trade Administration, Trade Development, Department of Commerce, 14th & Constitution Avenue NW, Washington, DC 20230. Phone (202) 377-1316.

22. SALES LEADS FROM OVERSEAS FIRMS

The **Trade Opportunities Program** (TOP) provides timely sales leads, joint ventures, and licensing opportunities from overseas firms and foreign governments seeking to buy or represent U.S. products and services. U.S. Commercial Officers worldwide gather leads through local channels.

Lead details, such as specifications, quantities, end-use, delivery, and bid deadlines, are delivered daily to Washington, and then made available electronically within 24 hours directly to the U.S. business community in both printed and electronic form through private sector nationwide distributors. Both new and established exporters can use TOP as a fundamental sales tool.

Contact: Trade Opportunities Program (TOP), International Trade Administration, United States and Foreign Commercial Service, Department of Commerce, 14th & Constitution Avenue NW, Washington DC 20230. Phone (202) 377-8246.

23. CREDIT AND OTHER INFO ON FOREIGN FIRMS

Two sources of background information on foreign firms are the World Traders Data Reports and the Eximbank.

a. The World Traders Data Reports (WTDRs) are provided on individual foreign firms, containing information about each firm's business activities, its standing in the local business community, its credit-worthiness, and its overall reliability and suitability as a trade contract for U.S. exporters.

WTDRs are designed to help U.S. firms locate and evaluate potential foreign customers before making a business commitment.

A typical WTDR includes: name, address, and key contact, numbers of employees, type of business, general reputation in trade and financial circles, an assessment of the firm's suitability as a trade contact, year established, sales territory, and products handled.

Compiled by U.S. Commercial Officers abroad, WTDRs reflect their knowledge of local firms and business practices and include an evaluation of a company's suitability as a trade contract. In addition to normal checks with banks, trade and financial references, corporate and public records, local credit agencies and customers, the embassy uses its own files and contacts to compile each report.

In many less developed countries, where even routine commercial information can be hard to get, WTDRs offer an excellent alternative to the difficult and painstaking task of acquiring information through individual contacts.

Contact: WTDRs, International Trade Administration, United States and Foreign Commercial Service, Department of Commerce, 14th & Constitution Avenue NW, Washington, DC 20230. Phone (202) 377-3181.

b. Credit information of exceptional value is also available from the Eximbank to the commercial banking community and U.S. exporting firms in the financing of export sales to a specific country or individual company abroad.

To date, this has been one of the many resources of the Export-Import Bank that has not been utilized to full advantage. In keeping with traditional business practices, Eximbank will not divulge confidential financial data on foreign buyers to whom it has extended credit, nor will it disclose classified or confidential information regarding particular credits or conditions in foreign countries. However, the experience as related to repayment records of companies or countries with which Eximbank has done business can have a definite bearing on a decision to pursue certain export transactions overseas.

In addition, Eximbank is in a position to obtain additional information through its association with the banking and exporting community and other international agencies whose reviews might be helpful in determining if the export financing project should be undertaken.

The principal targets in Eximbank's campaign to furnish good credit data are the smaller exporters and commercial banks with limited international trade facilities.

Contact: Export-Import Bank of the United States, 811 Vermont Avenue, N.W., Washington, DC 20571. Phone (202) 566-4690.

24. INFORMATION ON FISHERIES IN FOREIGN COUNTRIES

The **Foreign Fisheries Analysis Program** monitors the fisheries in every maritime nation. It collects, evaluates, and distributes information on the latest political, economic, and scientific developments in world fisheries that affects the U.S. fishing industry or U.S. Government policies and programs.

The branch also provides information concerning international aquaculture developments.

Contact: National and Oceanic and Atmospheric Administration, National Marine Fisheries Service, Department of Commerce, 1335 East-West Highway, Silver Spring, MD 20910. Phone (301) 443-8910.

25. DOMESTIC AND FOREIGN FISHERIES MARKET NEWS

The **Market News Program** offers current information on prices, market conditions, landings, imports, exports, cold-storage holdings, and market receipts of fishery products.

Information is collected by market reporters, and compiled and disseminated by Market News offices in Boston, New York, New Orleans, Terminal Island, and Seattle. The information aids U.S. buyers and sellers of fishery products in making intelligent marketing decisions.

Also reported is ancillary information such as innovations in harvesting, production, marketing, packaging and storage of fishery products, Federal fishery regulations and legislation, Regional Fishery Management Council meetings and activities, foreign fishing activities, foreign market information; and fishery meetings.

Contact: Market News Program, National Oceanic and Atmospheric Administration, National Marine Fisheries Service, Department of Commerce, 1335 East-West Highway, Silver Spring, MD 20910. Phone (301) 443-8910.

26. COUNSELING ON BI-NATIONAL TECHNOLOGICAL JOINT VENTURES

Information and counseling is available for those interested in establishing binational technology-oriented joint ventures. Experience with the successful U.S.-Israel bi-national **Industrial Research and Development Program** is used as the basis.

The service focuses on higher technology and smaller businesses which have little knowledge of how to expand into operations abroad.

Contact: International Operations, Office of Productivity, Department of Commerce, 14th & Constitution Avenue NW, Room 4816H, Washington, DC 20230. Phone Susan M. Lipsky at (202) 377-8014.

27. LEGAL ASSISTANCE ON DUTY REFUNDS

Refund assistance in the form of drawback is a provision of law by which a lawfully collected duty or tax is refunded or remitted, wholly or partially, because of a particular use made of the commodity on which the duty or tax was collected.

It encourages U.S. exporters by permitting them to compete in foreign markets without the handicap of including in the sales price the duty paid on the imported merchandise.

Since the exporter must know, before making contractual commitments, that he or she will be entitled to drawback on the exports, the drawback procedure is designed to give exporters this assurance and protection.

Drawback is payable to the exporter unless the manufacturer reserves the right to claim the refund. Several types of drawback are authorized under 19 U.S. C. 1313.

For more information, ask for the pamphlet *Drawback—A Duty Refund on Certain Exports* from any Government Printing Office bookstore or from the office below.

Contact: Entry Rulings Branch, U.S. Customs, Department of the Treasury, 1301 Constitution Avenue NW, Washington, DC 20229. Phone (202) 566-5856.

28. IF YOU'VE BEEN HURT BY UNFAIR FOREIGN TRADE PRACTICE

The **Trade Remedy Assistance Center** provides information on remedies and benefits available under trade laws and on the procedures necessary to obtain these benefits. For example, if you produce an item in competition with an item being imported and imports are increasing as to be a substantial cause of serious economic injury to the domestic market, a tariff adjustment or import quota may be imposed.

Affected firms and workers can also apply for financial assistance.

If a foreign government is subsidizing a product, you can petition for a countervailing duty to be imposed on the product. In 1987, 55 investigations of subsidies were performed.

If a foreign company is selling merchandise at less than fair value (dumping) in the U.S., anti-dumping duties may be imposed.

Contact: Trade Remedy Assistance Center, International Trade Commission, 500 E Street SW, Room 401, Washington, DC 20436. Phone (202) 252-2200.

29. INVESTMENT OPPORTUNITIES OVERSEAS

Two programs run by the Overseas Private Investment Corporation (a government agency) are the **Investor Information Service** and the **Opportunity Bank**.

For American businesses considering overseas ventures, obtaining basic information about foreign countries and their business environments is an important first step. Unfortunately, this is frequently a difficult and time-consuming process, given the variety of potential information sources and the resulting research required.

a. Investor Information Service

To assist U.S. firms in gathering such information, as well as facilitate the flow of information about developing countries to potential U.S. investors, OPIC has created the **Investor Information Service (IIS)**. IIS is a publications clearinghouse that provides interested companies and individuals with easy one-stop shopping for basic data and information commonly sought when considering investment overseas.

The materials, which are gathered into kit form, have been obtained from various U.S. Government agencies, foreign governments and international organizations. Together these source materials cover the economies, trade laws, business regulations and attitudes, political conditions, and investment incentives of specific developing countries and areas.

The information kits packaged by IIS are categorized by individual countries as well as major geographic regions. At present, IIS kits are available for more than 100 developing countries and 10 regions.

b. Opportunity Bank

A major stumbling block in the Third World's attempt to attract U.S. investment capital arises from the limited flow of information between potential U.S. equity investors and likely sponsors of investment projects in the developing countries. In its continuing effort to promote U.S. direct investment in the developing nations, OPIC has sought to establish channels of investment information by developing a computerized data system called the **Opportunity Bank**.

The primary purpose of this data bank is to enable U.S. firms and overseas project sponsors to register their respective investment interests and requirements, thus permitting rapid access to this information by interested potential joint-venture partners in the United States and abroad.

Currently, the Opportunity Bank contains more than 1,000 investment project profiles on a broad cross-section of potential joint-venture enterprises in more than 75 countries in the developing world. The company file contains more than 4,000 potential U.S. investors.

For more information on these programs, contact: Overseas Private Investment Corporation, 1615 M Street NW, Washington, DC 20527. Phone (800) 424-6742. For businesses in Washington, DC call (202) 457-7010.

30. FOREIGN-TRADE ZONES IN THE UNITED STATES

Exporters should consider the use of foreign trade zones located in over 35 communities in the U.S. These zones are considered outside customs territory.

Activities such as storage, assembly, inspection, and repacking, which might otherwise be carried on overseas, are permitted.

For export operations the zones provide accelerated export status for excise tax rebates and customs drawbacks.

Contact: Office of Executive Secretary, Foreign Trade Zones Board, Room 1529, 14th & Pennsylvania Ave. NW, Washington, DC 20230. Phone John DaPonte at (202) 377-2862.

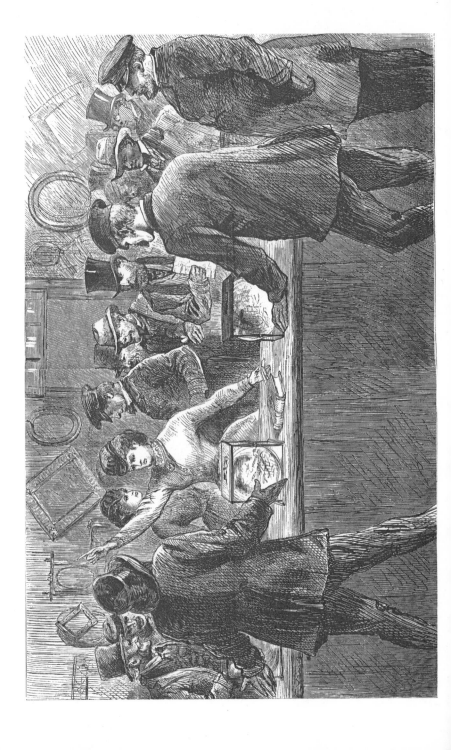

Chapter 9

WOMEN, MINORITIES, AND DISADVANTAGED

1. SHORT-TERM LENDING AND BONDING ASSISTANCE

The **Minority Business Resource Center** of the Department of Transportation operates two programs for minority, women-owned, and disadvantaged business enterprises:

a. The Short-Term Lending Program, which provides short-term working capital at prime interest rates for transportation-related projects.

b. The Bonding Assistance Program, which enables businesses to obtain bids, payment, and performance bonds for transportation-related projects.

For a minimal fee, these programs will also assist in the loan packaging.

Contact: Office of Small and Disadvantaged Business Utilization (OSDBU), Department of Transportation, Minority Business Resource Center, 400 7th Street SW, Room 9410, Washington, DC 20590. Phone (202) 366-2852.

2. INFORMATION NETWORKS

A nationwide **Business Information Network** has been established by the Minority Business Development Agency of the Department of Commerce. It collects and disseminates information that is of special importance to the successful establishment and operation of minority business.

The Network is comprised of 100 Minority Business Development Centers throughout the country, and the MBDA Information Clearinghouse Center.

The Centers are linked together through a telecommunications network and use remote terminals to access automated business information systems.

Information Clearinghouse

Services available from the Clearinghouse are:

a. Referral to sources of management and technical assistance for minority entrepreneurs.

b. Identification of minority vendors for government agency procurement opportunities.

c. Statistics and reports on Agency performance.

d. Information about the Agency and other Federal support of minority assistance programs.

e. Referral to and use of information resources at the Clearinghouse Reference Room.

Business Development Centers

Resources available through the Business Development Centers are:

a. The Minority Vendor PROFILE System, which is a computerized inventory of non-retail minority firms used for matching companies with opportunities.

b. The X/Market database containing information on approximately 500,000 U.S. establishments in more than 950 industries, used in making decisions concerning marketing, sales and research.

c. Dun and Bradstreet Information Systems, which provides detailed financial profiles and computations useful in evaluating the performance of companies.

d. DMS/ONLINE Information Systems which contains information on U.S. Government prime contract awards and plans for defense and aerospace programs and for identifying direct subcontracting opportunities for minority businesses.

e. The TECTRA database that identifies new technologies being used in the public sector that are thus available for commercialization.

f. The Donnelly X/Census Plus database that identifies desired characteristics of a given marketing location, and can also be searched to identify a location that meets these characteristics.

g. The Federal Procurement Data System reports on various aspects of Federal procurement activities showing historical data on what the U.S. Government buys, used by many firms to develop marketing strategies.

h. The F. W. Dodge Construction Information subscription service that provides information to minority business persons on both private and public sector construction opportunities, including post-construction services such as maintenance and landscaping.

More than 100 Minority Business Development Centers, located in areas across the country with the largest minority populations, are funded to provide management, marketing, and technical assistance to increase business opportunities for minority entrepreneurs in the United States and foreign markets.

Each center can assist existing firms as well as minority individuals interested in starting a business, and minimize their business failures.

The centers provide vital accounting, administration, business planning, construction, and marketing information. The sources of the information are major U.S. corporations, trade associations, export management companies, and Federal, state and local government agencies.

They also identify minority-owned firms for contract and sub-contract opportunities with Federal, state and local government agencies and the private sector. Some of the services include: financial statement compilation; cost accounting; budgeting; tax planning; loan proposals; cash forecasting; office management; form design; management development; job evaluation; performance reviews feasibility studies; long-range planning; pre-merger analysis; operation analysis construction bonding and estimating; bid preparation; pricing policies; advertising; promotion; consumer surveys; and merchandising.

Businesses should contact their nearest MBDA regional office. To find it look in the telephone book or contact Minority Business Development Agency, Department of Commerce, 14th & Constitution Avenue NW, Washington, DC 20230. Phone (202) 377-2414.

3. TELECOMMUNICATIONS OPPORTUNITIES FOR MINORITIES

Engineering and management assistance is provided by the **Minority Telecommunications Development Program** to increase minority participation in all phases of telecommunications.

Through this program, minority business persons, educational institutions, and organizations are assisted in the creation and expansion of telecommunications businesses.

The MTDP helps minority entrepreneurs through a variety of initiatives:

(1) providing through its broadcast technical services project, initial engineering assistance in starting a broadcast facility;

(2) analyzing and participating in industry developments, legislative and regulatory policymaking, and FCC proceedings to ensure that policies will adequately consider minority interests;

(3) holding seminars and briefing for minority entrepreneurs and other organizations interested in business, manufacturing, and ownership opportunities available in telecommunications.

The MTDP has developed three kits — commercial, noncommercial, and new technologies — to explain the services provided and also to inform minorities of the options and resources available in developing a telecommunications business. The kits provide: Information on the Technical Planning Services (TPS) component which assists minority entrepreneurs in the initial steps of developing commercial and noncommercial television and radio stations; information handouts on starting commercial television and radio stations, cable systems, and a model financial proposal for the entrepreneur; fact sheets on opportunities in the newer technologies; sources for funding opportunities and technical assistance; and directors and general listings on assistance available.

Contact: Minority Telecommunications Development Program, National Telecommunications and Information Administration, Department of Commerce, 14th & Constitution Avenue NW, Room 4890H, Washington, DC 20230. Phone (202) 377-1835.

4. ENERGY-RELATED OPPORTUNITIES FOR MINORITIES

The **National Minority Energy Information Clearinghouse** is a centralized repository and dissemination point for energy-related research data and information about energy programs and the economic impact of those programs on minorities, minority businesses, and minority educational institutions. Information is provided about the Department of Energy (DOE) and the Office of Minority Economic Impact's (MI) Programs.

The clearinghouse maintains a database and provides searches and specialized information that is available through linkages with other databases of other Federal agencies.

Services available from the clearinghouse are:

(1) Referrals to sources of management and an array of technical assistance to minority business enterprises and minority educational institutions and to sources for procurement and research opportunities.

(2) Identification of minority vendors for government procurement opportunities.

(3) Statistics and performance reports on the Department's activities with minority educational institutions and minority business enterprises.

(4) Information about DOE and other Federal agencies' support of minority assistance programs.

(5) Identification of the research in progress in the Department.

(6) Information on the impact of energy policies and programs on minorities.

(7) Regional information on socio-economic and demographic data on minorities and their energy use patterns, and

(8) Referrals to sources which assist in energy development programs for minority communities.

Contact: Minority Economic Impact Office, Department of Energy, 1000 Independence Avenue SW, Room 5B-110, Washington, DC 20585. Phone (202) 586-5876.

5. BUSINESS LOANS AND GRANTS FOR INDIANS AND ALASKA NATIVES

The **Bureau of Indian Affairs** will provide grants, direct loans and guaranteed loans for business, agriculture, industry and housing for Indians, Alaska natives, and Indian organizations.

Any purpose that will promote economic development on or near a Federal Indian Reservation will be considered. In 1989 approximately $12 million is available for loan guarantees. Some recent projects were construction of a Dairy Queen, a cabinet factory, and a fish processing plant.

In addition, seed money in the form of grants up to $100,000 to individuals or $250,000 to tribes is available for profit-oriented business enterprises. One recent grant was for $40,000 to purchase a pizza parlor. The business is flourishing and they have expanded into a second restaurant without government assistance.

Contact: Trust and Economic Development, Bureau of Indian Affairs, 18th & C Street NW, Room 4600, Washington, DC 20240. Or phone Ray Quinn at (202) 343-5831.

6. GRANTS FOR ENERGY USAGE RESEARCH

Money is available for research of **minority** energy usage such as: studies of the percentage of disposable income spent by minorities on energy compared to national averages, establishing consumption and usage patterns, and assessing potential policies and programs to be implemented by legislative and regulatory agencies.

Small and disadvantaged businesses in energy related fields are encouraged to apply.

Contact: Department of Energy, Forrestal Building Room 5B-110, Washington, DC 20585. Phone Georgia R. Johnson at (202) 586-1593.

7. HOW TO CONTACT OFFICES OF SMALL AND DISADVANTAGED BUSINESS UTILIZATION (OSDBUs)

Department of Agriculture

The procurement procedures of the Department are explained by contacting the office. A special publication contains information on who does the buying, the types of items bought for the various programs, and where the buying is done. Included is a directory of purchasing offices and their locations.

Copies are available from this office. Information about contracting and subcontracting opportunities is also provided.

Contact: OSDBU, Department of Agriculture, 14th & Independence Avenue SW, Room 124-W, Washington, DC 20250. Phone (202) 447-7117.

Department of Commerce

The OSDBU office helps small and disadvantaged businesses to a fair share of Government procurement opportunities. If a company qualifies, the office provides Commerce procurement offices with copies of the company's capability statement.

These statements are used to develop source lists for their future purchases, which could mean increased sales for firms. A capability statement can be brief — two to five pages — but it should contain: a statement of a firm's strategy, philosophy or purpose; a list of past and present clients and references; a summary of the firm's marketing experience.

It is also useful to include: a list of the firm's principals and their resumés; a description of the firm's specialty areas; Commerce Department activities that especially interest you.

Contact: OSDBU, Department of Commerce, Room H6411, 14th & Constitution Avenue NW, Washington, DC 20230. Phone Mr. James P. Maruca at (202) 377-3387.

Department of Defense

The OSDBU office is the starting point for small businesses, small disadvantaged businesses, labor surplus, and women-owned business firms desiring to do business with DOD.

A series of publications are available to lead a business to the right contacts with the large DOD procurement system. The key publications available include: *Selling to the Military*, *Department of Defense Small Business and Labor-Surplus Area Specialists*, and *Small Business Subcontracting Directory*.

Contact: OSDBU, Department of Defense, Room 2A340, The Pentagon, Washington, DC 20301-3061. Phone (202) 697-1481.

Department of Education

The procurement procedures of the Department are explained by contacting the OSDBU office.

A special publication contains information on who does the buying, the types of items bought for the various programs, and where the buying is done. Included is a directory of purchasing offices and their locations. Copies are available from this office.

Contact: OSDBU, Department of Education, Room 4329, 330 C Street SW, Washington, DC 20202-2410. Phone (202) 732-4500.

Department of Energy

The OSDBU office is the advocate and point of contact for small, disadvantaged (including 8a certified firms), labor surplus areas and women-owned businesses.

The office counsels such firms on how to do business with the department. They also provide the names of small/disadvantaged business specialists located in the procurement offices throughout the country who can supply more specific requirement information. Preference programs are explained and potential vendors are referred to appropriate program offices.

Contact: OSDBU, Department of Energy, MA-41, 1000 Independence Avenue SW, Washington, DC 20585. Phone (202) 586-8201.

Department of Health and Human Services

The OSDBU office develops and implements appropriate outreach programs aimed at heightening the awareness of the small business community to the contracting opportunities available within the Department.

Outreach efforts include activities such as sponsoring small business fairs and procurement conferences as well as participating in trade group seminars, conventions, and other forums which promote the utilization of small and disadvantaged businesses as contractors.

The OSDBU provides counseling and advice to inquiring small businesses regarding their possible eligibility for special consideration under preferential procurement programs for the Department employs.

Contact: OSDBU, Department of Health and Human Services, Room 513-D HHH, 200 Independence Avenue SW, Washington, DC 20201. Phone (202) 245-7300.

Department of Housing and Urban Development (HUD)

The OSDBU office helps small, minority, and women-owned businesses understand HUD's operations and directs offerors to appropriate sources of information. OSDBU works with program offices throughout the Department to develop goals for Procurement Opportunity Programs (POPs), Minority Business Enterprises (MBEs), and to encourage implementation of subcontracting plans for small and disadvantaged businesses.

It provides advice to contracting officers in complying with small and disadvantaged business utilization plans. The office participates in government/industry conferences to assist small and disadvantaged businesses and is available to give direct advice, as it is needed.

In addition, the office sponsors seminars and presentations at appropriate trade shows, conferences, and policy sessions.

OSDBU develops the Department's annual Minority Business Development Plan to encourage greater participation by minority business enterprises in all HUD programs.

Contact: OSDBU, Department of Housing and Urban Development, Room 10226, 451 Seventh Street SW, Washington, DC 20410. Phone (202) 755-1428.

Department of Justice

The OSDBU office develops and implements appropriate outreach programs aimed at heightening the awareness of the small business community to the contracting opportunities available within the Department.

Outreach efforts include activities such as sponsoring small business fairs and procurement conferences as well as participating in trade group seminars, conventions, and other forums which promote the utilization of small businesses as contractors.

The OSDBU also provides counseling and advice to inquiring small businesses regarding their possible eligibility for special consideration under preferential purchasing programs which the Department employs.

Contact: OSDBU, Department of Justice, 10th Street and Pennsylvania Avenue NW, Washington, DC 20530. Phone (202) 724-6271.

Department of Labor

The department places a fair proportion of its private sector purchases and contracts for supplies, research and development, and services (including contracts for maintenance, repairs, and construction) with small business and small disadvantaged business concerns.

The OSDBU office promotes opportunities for small business and disadvantaged business concerns in acquisition programs, disseminates information about those laws administered by the Department which affect contractor and subcontractor operations, and provides assistance to small and disadvantaged business concerns either directly or through coordinated interdepartmental activities.

The procurement procedures of the Department are explained in a publication titled *What the U.S. Department of Labor Buys*. This publication contains information on who does the buying, the types of items bought for the various programs, and where the buying is done. Included is a directory of purchasing offices and their locations. A copy is available from this office.

Contact: OSDBU, Department of Labor, Room S-1004, 200 Constitution Avenue NW, Washington, DC 20210. Phone (202) 523-9148.

Department of the Interior

The OSDBU office is the central point of contact for small businesses, small disadvantaged businesses, labor surplus, and woman-owned business firms desiring to do business with the Department. The office is prepared to discuss the various preference programs and can assist firms in contacting appropriate Department offices.

Contact: OSDBU, Department of the Interior, 18th & C Street NW, Washington, DC 20240. Phone (202) 343-8493.

NASA

The OSDBU office (Code K) is responsible for the development and management of NASA programs to assist small businesses, as well as firms which are owned and controlled by socially and economically disadvantaged individuals.

The office functionally oversees and directs the activities of corresponding offices at each installation.

The primary objective of the program is to increase the participation of small and disadvantaged businesses in NASA procurement.

The office offers individual counseling sessions to business people seeking advice on how to best pursue contracting opportunities with NASA.

Specific guidance is provided regarding procedures for getting on the bidders mailing lists, current and planned procurement opportunities, arrangements for meetings with technical requirements personnel, and various assistance or preference programs which might be available.

Contact: OSDBU, National Aeronautics and Space Administration, Code K, Washington, DC 20546. Phone Mr. Eugene D. Rosen at (202) 453-2088.

Department of Transportation

The OSDBU office provides assistance, referrals, and business opportunity information resulting from the Department's federally assisted projects to minority and women business enterprises through its nationwide Program Management Center Project, Hispanic Business Enterprise Project, and National Information Clearinghouse.

It provides assistance in obtaining short-term capital and bonding for minority and women business enterprises.

The MBRC contracts annually with a number of organizations to assist minority and women business enterprises in obtaining contracts from federally assisted projects.

Contact: OSDBU, Department of Transportation, Room 9410, 400 7th Street SW, Washington, DC 20590. Phone (202) 366-2852.

Department of the Treasury

The OSDBU office is a central point of contact for small business, small disadvantaged business, labor surplus and women-owned business firms desiring to do business with the Treasury.

OSDBU is prepared to discuss the various procurement programs and can assist firms in contacting appropriate Treasury procurement personnel.

Contact: OSDBU, Department of the Treasury, Main Treasury Building, 15th and Pennsylvania Ave. NW, Washington, DC 20220. Phone Ms. Debra E. Sonderman at (202) 566-9272.

Chapter 10

ODDS AND ENDS

1. ANSWERS TO QUESTIONS ON TRUTH IN ADVERTISING, MAIL ORDER, BUYING BY PHONE

The **Public Reference Branch** of the Federal Trade Commission answers questions concerning truthful advertising, price fixing, product warranties, truth in lending, and other unfair and deceptive business acts. It offers business assistance in learning about current regulations and enforcement procedures.

Examples of common questions answered include: mail orders rules, buying by phone, FTC used car rules, getting business credit, handling customer complaints, how to advertise consumer credit, making business sense out of warranty law, and writing a care label.

Although major emphasis is placed on correcting unfair or deceptive business practices that hurt competition, businesses can also inform the Commission of unfair competition from monopolistic practices including price fixing, boycotts, price discrimination, and illegal mergers and acquisitions.

Ten regional FTC offices also have been established to assist businesses and consumers.

Contact: Public Reference Branch, Federal Trade Commission, Room 130, 6th & Pennsylvania Avenue NW, Washington, DC 20580. Phone (202) 326-2222.

2. BUYING SURPLUS GOODS

The National Defense Stockpile Office acquires and retains certain materials in order to prevent a dependence upon foreign nations in times of national emergency. Disposals are made when materials in inventory are found to be in excess of national security needs and—usually—are approved by Congress.

Disposals are conducted on a nonexclusive, nondiscriminatory basis by means of sealed bids, auctions, negotiations, or other sales methods.

Every reasonable effort is made to carry out a long-term acquisition and disposal plan as formally announced. This allows industry to make developmental, research, and investment plans in anticipation of these disposals.

Contact: National Defense Stockpile Office, General Services Administration, 18th & F Street NW, Washington, DC 20405. Phone (202) 535-7224.

3. BUYING SURPLUS REAL ESTATE

The Federal Property Resource Service of the General Services Administration has the principal responsibility for surplus real property sales. It sells nearly every type of real estate found on the commercial market.

In many cases, buyers may use the properties immediately after they have been awarded the contract for purchase.

When Government real property is for sale, the GSA regional office prepares a notice describing the property and how it will be sold. The notice is mailed to those who have shown an interest in buying similar property.

A computerized mailing list is maintained, and bidders' applications are available at each of GSA's Business Service Centers.

Contact: Federal Property Resource Service, General Services Administration, Office of Real Property, Washington, DC 20405. Phone (202) 535-7067.

4. COMMODITY FUTURES AND HOW THEY CAN BE USED TO CONTROL COSTS

The Communications and Education Services Office of the Commodity Futures Trading Commission offers information about commodity futures and options to make sure that businesses do not overlook their value in company purchasing and marketing strategies.

Although only a small percentage of futures trading actually leads to delivery of a commodity, futures trading can be a valuable cost control method for companies.

The Commission regulates trading, offers information about futures, and works with business groups on new contracts or rule changes and to help educate them about these changes.

Contact: The Communication and Education Service Office, Commodity Futures Trading Commission, 2033 K Street NW, Washington, DC 20581. Phone (202) 254-6387.

5. MANAGEMENT ASSISTANCE FOR RURAL CO-OPS

The Agricultural Cooperative Service provides research, management, and educational assistance to cooperatives to strengthen the economic position of farmers and other rural residents.

It works directly with cooperative leaders and Federal and State agencies to improve organization, leadership, and operation of cooperatives and to give guidance to further development.

It (1) helps farmers and other rural residents develop cooperatives to obtain supplies and services at lower costs and to get better prices for products they sell; (2) advises rural residents on developing existing resources through cooperative action to enhance rural living; (3) helps cooperatives improve services and operating efficiency; (4) informs members, directors, employers, and the public on how co-operatives work and benefit their members and their communities; and (5) encourages international cooperative programs.

The agency publishes research and educational materials, and issues *Farmer Cooperatives*, a monthly periodical.

Contact: Agricultural Cooperative Service, Department of Agriculture, Washington, DC 20250. Phone Dr. Randall E. Tongenson at (202) 653-6977.

6. WHERE TO GET ANSWERS ON ENERGY CONSERVATION AND CREATING RENEWABLE ENERGY FROM WIND, SUN, CROPS AND WASTE

The Conservation and Renewable Energy Inquiry and Referral Service (CAREIRS) provides basic information on the full spectrum of renewable energy technologies — solar, wind, hydroelectric, photovoltaics, geothermal and bioconversion — and on energy conservation.

For requesters who need detailed assistance on technical problems, CAREIRS provides referrals to other organizations or publications. Its purpose is to aid technology transfer by responding to public inquiries on the use of renewable energy technologies and conservation techniques for residential and commercial needs.

Once an inquiry has been initiated, the response process is basically computerized. Responses consist of a form letter with applicable publications; an immediate telephone response; an occasional original draft response; or referral to other organizations.

Contact: CAREIRS, Department of Energy, P. O. Box 8900, Silver Spring, MD 20907. Call toll-free (800) 523-2929, in Alaska and Hawaii call (800) 233-3071.

7. HELP WITH LABOR MANAGEMENT RELATIONS

Two programs can provide timely information and help.

The first one is the **Cooperative Labor Management Program**, often identified as the Quality of Work Life program. It is a joint effort by labor and management to work together to further their mutual interests. The aim is more satisfied and involved employees and more efficient, adaptive, and productive organizations.

The program offers a wide range of information and technical assistance services including the sponsorship of conferences and symposia, the publication of reports on organizational experiences, the preparation of educational and training materials, and the conduct of research and evaluation studies.

There is particular interest in gathering and disseminating information about innovative policies and programs developed to enhance employee participation in decision-making with regard to such issues as work organization, the work environment, technological change, and plant closures.

The division works primarily with national unions, trade associations, productivity and quality of work life centers, colleges and universities, and other organizations interested in cooperative labor relations and quality of work life programs.

For more information on this, contact: Cooperative Labor-Management Program, Department of Labor, 200 Constitution Avenue NW, Room N-5416, Washington, DC 20210. Phone (202) 523-6098.

The second program is the **Mediation and Conciliation Service**, which promotes labor-management peace and better labor-management relations by providing mediation assistance in disputes arising between organized employees and their employers. The service has 80 field offices in cities across the United States.

Businesses will find its services helpful in preventing or minimizing work stoppages; in helping to resolve collective bargaining disputes, by creating a better degree of understanding and cooperation between management and labor; and in assisting labor and management to select impartial arbitrators to hear and decide disputes over collective bargaining agreements.

In general, assistance from the service is limited to domestic employers involved in interstate commerce and to related labor organizations. Except as a last resort, it refrains from participation in intrastate matters or in controversies pertaining to the interpretation or application of existing contracts. Services may be provided either upon notice required by law or at the request of the involved parties.

The labor organizations involved must be recognized by the National Labor Relations Board as legitimate representatives of employee groups.

A series of films is also available. They illustrate many of today's labor relations problems.

Contact: Labor Mediation and Conciliation Services, Washington, DC 20427. Phone Mr. Dennis Minshall at (202) 653-5300.

8. YOUR FRIEND IN THE ENVIRONMENTAL PROTECTION AGENCY

The EPA Small Business Ombudsman has the mission of providing small businesses with easier access to the Agency; helping them comply with environmental regulations; investigating and resolving small business disputes with the Agency; increasing EPA's sensitivity to small business in developing regulations; dealing with EPA enforcement policies, inspection procedures, and fines; understanding water-permitting regulations and requirements for handling and treating hazardous wastes; complying with registration procedures for pesticides; and information on financing for pollution control equipment.

They answer all kinds of questions, too. For instance, want to import an automobile? Ask them about emissions requirements. Need some bacterial cultures for lab research? They'll send some from their lab. Can't understand the government's EPA rules? They'll have one of their people walk you through it.

A major responsibility of the Ombudsman is to follow closely the status and development of EPA policies affecting small businesses. The Ombudsman's office can help provide the latest information on new regulations. Several EPA brochures and reports on various small business activities and environmental issues also are available.

Contact: EPA Small Business Ombudsman, Environmental Protection Agency, 401 M Street SW (A-149C), Washington, DC 20460. Call Karen V. Brown toll-free at (800) 368-5888, or in Washington DC (202) 557-1938.

9. IMPARTIAL INFORMATION ON PESTICIDES

The National Pesticide Telecommunications Network provides a variety of impartial information about pesticides to anyone in the contiguous United States, Puerto Rico, and the Virgin Islands. It provides the medical community health professional with: pesticide product information; information on recognition and management of poisonings; and toxicology and symptomatic reviews. It also give referrals for: laboratory analyses, investigations of pesticide incidents, and emergency treatment information.

The general public is also provided pesticide information ranging from: product information, protective equipment, safety, health and environmental effects, clean-up procedures, disposal, regulatory laws, etc.

Contact: National Pesticides Telecommunications Network, Environmental Protection Agency, Texas Tech University, Health Sciences Center, Department of Preventive Medicine, Lubbock, TX 79430. Call toll-free (800) 858-7378.

10. ASSISTANCE CONCERNING HAZARDOUS WASTES

The Hazardous Waste/Superfund Hotline was created because the Environmental Protection Agency recognized: (1) that many of the firms which must comply with regulations would have difficulty understanding the regulations and the statutory requirements; (2) that many of these firms, particularly the smaller ones, were not in a financial position to hire consultants to answer their compliance questions; and (3) that interested communities, including private citizens, may have questions.

The Hotline serves as a central source of technical information on the Superfund Program and the Hazardous Waste Management Program.

The Hotline responds to approximately 8,000 calls per month on regulations and program activities. In addition, the Hotline telephone service accepts requests for related publications. When additional information is required, the Hotline refers callers to appropriate contacts at EPA Headquarters, EPA Regional offices, and other Federal and state agencies. The Hotline telephone staff has ten information specialists with background in geology, chemistry, chemical and environmental engineering, hydrogeology, biology, and environmental science.

Contact: Hazardous Wastes/Superfund Hotline, Environmental Protection Agency, 401 M Street SW, Mail Code WH562A, Washington, DC 20460. Call toll-free (800) 424-9346 or in Washington, DC (202) 382-3000.

11. CRIME INSURANCE FOR SMALL BUSINESSES

The Federal Crime Insurance Program makes crime insurance available in states where it has been determined that this insurance is not fully available at affordable rates.

This federally subsidized program was created to make crime insurance more readily available in areas where people have been unable to buy or renew crime insurance protection from the private insurance market. Policies normally will not be cancelled or non-renewed because the policyholder has reported losses.

Coverage for business is available in increments of $1,000 up to a maximum of $15,000 with a choice of the following policy coverage:

Option 1: Burglary only, including safe burglary, and resulting damage.

Option 2: Robbery only, inside and away from the premises, and resulting damage.

Option 3: A combination of burglary and robbery in uniform and varying amounts.

Contact: Federal Crime Insurance Program, Federal Insurance Administration, Federal Emergency Management Agency, P O Box 6301, Rockville, MD 20850. Call toll-free (800) 638-8780; businesses in Washington, DC or Maryland should call (301) 251-1660.

12. COMPUTER SOFTWARE YOU CAN HAVE

The Computer Software and Management Information Center (COSMIC) makes available to business and industry over 1,200 computer programs covering all areas of NASA project involvement, including structural analysis, thermal engineering, computer graphics, image processing, controls and robotics, artificial intelligence and expert systems. Source code is supplied for each program along with detailed user documentation.

Contact: COSMIC, National Aeronautics and Space Administration, University of Georgia, 382 E. Broad St., Athens, GA 30602. Phone (404) 542-3265.

13. AUDIO VISUAL PROGRAMS AVAILABLE FOR YOU

The National Audiovisual Center is the central distribution source of audiovisual programs produced by the U.S. Government. Companies interested in using video material for training will find it useful to obtain copies of the center's descriptive catalogs and brochures.

Some of the audiovisuals available cover: alcohol and drug abuse, business/government management, consumer education, dentistry, environment/energy conservation, flight/meteorology, foreign language instruction, history, industrial safety, library/information science, medicine, nursing, science, social issues, special education, and vocational education.

Contact: National Audiovisual Center, National Archives and Records Administration, 8700 Edgeworth Drive, Capitol Heights, MD 20743. Phone (301) 763-1896.

14. HELP FOR BUSINESSES IN PROTECTING PENSION PLANS

The Communications and Public Affairs Department of the Pension Benefit Guaranty Corporation (PBGC) will explain how the PBGC protects the retirement incomes of more than thirty eight million American workers participating in more than 112,000 covered private-sector benefit pension plans.

The Corporation has assumed liability for payment of guaranteed vested pension benefits to more than 193,000 participants in approximately 1,400 plans that have terminated and are or will be trusteed by the PBGC, and is currently paying monthly retirement benefits to more than

184,000 retirees. The amount of the monthly benefit that the PBGC guarantees is set by law.

The PBGC administers two pension programs: the single-employer program and the multi-employer program. The single-employer program covers approximately thirty million participants in about 110,000 single-employer pension plans.

When a single-employer plan insured by the PBGC terminates without sufficient funds to pay PBGC-guaranteed benefits, the PBGC makes up the difference, thus ensuring that all qualified participants and beneficiaries receive their guaranteed pensions.

The PBGC also assumes trusteeship of the plan and manages its assets, maintains the plan's records, and administers guaranteed benefits. The multi-employer program protects about eight million participants in more than 2,000 plans. Multi-employer pension plans are maintained under collective bargaining agreements and cover employees of two or more unrelated employers.

If PBGC-covered multi-employer plans become insolvent, they receive financial assistance from the PBGC to enable them to pay guaranteed benefits.

Contact: Communications and Public Affairs Department, Pension Benefit Guaranty Corporation, 2020 K Street NW, Washington, DC 20006-1806. Phone Mr. E. William FitzGerald at (202) 778-8839.

15. HOW TO REQUEST SECURITIES AND EXCHANGE COMMISSION INFORMATION

The Reference Assistance Program makes available Securities and Exchange Commission information collected when exercising its mandate concerning the protection of investors and the maintenance of fair and orderly securities markets. The Commission carries out its mandate under five principal laws. Under these Acts and the rules under them, publicly held corporations, broker-dealers in securities, investment companies and investment advisors must file information with the Commission. Filings are designed to ensure that all material information is available to the investing public in a timely fashion.

To ensure easy public access, the Commission maintains public reference rooms in New York, Chicago and in the headquarters office in Washington. During normal business hours, individuals may review and photocopy all public filings.

In addition, copies may be ordered by writing to the Commission or telephoning the Commission's contract copying service. The Commission will, upon written request, have copies of any public documents or information sent by mail. Companies or individuals must submit a written request stating the documents or information needed.

Further information should be obtained before writing and stating your willingness to pay the photocopying and shipping charges. Each request will take approximately two to three weeks for delivery.

For quicker service or in-depth research, it is suggested to employ one of the private firms which provide SEC research services. A list of these firms and additional information is available.

Contact: Reference Assistance Program, Securities and Exchange Commission, Public Reference Branch, Stop 1-2, 450 5th Street NW, Washington, DC 20549. Phone (202) 272-7450.

16. WHEN SOMEONE COMPLAINS ABOUT YOUR BUSINESS

The Office of Consumer Affairs provides assistance to businesses to help them improve customer relations. They have five consumer affairs guides for business: *Advertising, Packaging, and Labeling*; *Managing Consumer Complaints*; *Product Warranties and Services*; *Credit and Financial Issues*; and *Consumer Product Safety*.

They also present workshops based on these guides and have prepared manuals for use by the workshop coor-

dinators and consumer protection agencies. Other publications useful to businesses are *Consumer Services Directory* and *Guide to Complaint Handling*.

To get more information, write or call: Office of Consumer Affairs, John M. Gibbons, Director, Department of Commerce, Office of the Secretary, Washington, DC 20230. Phone (202) 377-5001.

17. HOW TO GET HELP ON SAFETY WITHOUT GETTING IN TROUBLE

Employers can receive a free confidential consultation to help recognize and correct safety and health hazards in their workplaces.

The service is delivered by a well-trained professional staff. Most consultations take place on-site, though limited services away from the worksite are available. Primarily targeted for smaller businesses, this confidential safety and health consultation program is completely separate from the OSHA inspection effort. In addition, no citations are issued or penalties imposed.

A consultant will study an entire plant or specific designated operations and discuss the applicable OSHA standards. Consultants also will point out other safety or health risks which might not be cited under OSHA standards, but which nevertheless may pose safety or health risks. They may suggest other measures such as self-inspection and safety and health training to prevent future hazardous situations.

A comprehensive consultation also includes:

(1) Appraisal of all mechanical and environmental hazards and physical work practices.

(2) Appraisal of the present job safety and health program or establishment of one.

(3) A conference with management on findings.

(4) A written report of recommendations and agreements.

(5) Training and assistance with implementing recommendations.

Contact: OSHA Consultation Program, Occupational Safety and Health Administration, Department of Labor, Room N-3700, 200 Constitution Avenue NW, Washington, DC 20210. Phone (202) 523-7266.

Appendix 1

USEFUL NONGOVERNMENT BUSINESS ASSOCIATIONS

Write or call to get information on the associations' latest programs. To reach other associations that pertain to your subject, call the American Society of Association Executives at (202) 626-2747. They can identify the ones you're interested in. Their address is 1575 I St. N.W., Washington, DC 20005.

1. **The Small Business Foundation of America** is the only independent research and education foundation on small business issues. They sponsor studies, publications, and public awareness programs. They publish *Exportise*; *Planning for Technology*; *How to Start and Continue a Small Business Trade Association*.

Small Business Foundation of America
20 Park Plaza, Suite 438
Boston, MA 02116
Phone Regina Tracy at (617) 350-5096.

2. The **Center for Family Business**, founded in 1962, is the oldest organization dedicated to providing family business owners and their families with research, publications,

seminars, and consulting on managing succession in the family business. They publish several books dealing with these issues.

Center for Family Business
P. O. Box 24268
5862 Mayfield Road
Cleveland, OH 44124
Phone Leon A. Danco, Ph.D., President, at (216) 442-0800

3. The **Center for Entrepreneurial Management** gives seminars nationwide featuring recognized experts and publishes the *Entrepreneurial Manager's Newsletter*, several dozen books and some audio tapes. Membership is $96 a year, which includes their newsletter, several books and tapes and subscriptions to *Inc.*, *Venture*, and *Success*.

CEM
180 Varick St.
Penthouse
New York, NY 10014-4606
Phone (212) 633-0060
Toll-free order line is 1-800-247-7642
Joseph R. Macuso, President

4. The **National Federation of Independent Business**, was founded in 1943 and is the nation's largest advocacy organization. NFIB advances the concerns of small-business owners to legislators.

NFIB uses direct balloting of its membership to determine policies and caps dues at $1,000 to prevent undue influence by any one member.

NFIB caseworkers provide individual answers to member inquiries on legislation and troubleshoot for members by dealing directly with appropriate agencies. NFIB in addition to its federal offices, has state legislative offices in all 50 states.

NFIB

Administrative Offices
150 W. 20th Ave.
San Mateo, CA 94403
Phone (415) 341-7441

NFIB
Government Relations
600 Maryland Ave. SW, Suite 700
Washington, DC 20024
Phone (202) 554-9000

5. The **U.S. Hispanic Chamber of Commerce** has national programs to assist hispanics, regional networking meetings, international trade contacts in Latin America, and vendor matching assistance with major corporations.

U. S. Hispanic Chamber of Commerce
Board of Trade Center
4900 Main
Kansas City, MO 64112
Phone Vincent Hamon at (816) 531-6363

6. The **Association of Collegiate Entrepreneurs** and **Young Entrepreneurs Organization** are international networking organizations dedicated to providing credibility and contacts for young-minded entrepreneurs. There is no age limit on membership. They seek to provide opportunities for student entrepreneurial pursuits by creating mentor relationships with business leaders. They have an annual convention and trade show. A monthly newsletter subscription is $15 a year. Membership is $24 a year, which includes the newsletter.

The Young Entrepreneurs Organization consists of entrepreneurs under the age of 30 with annual sales over $1 million.

Association of Collegiate Entrepreneurs
Center for Entrepreneurship
Box 147
Wichita State University

Wichita, KS 67208
Phone Donald Herman, Associate Director, at (316) 689-3000

7. The **International Council for Small Business**. The International Council's principal objective is to advance management practices of existing small business owners and potential entrepreneurs through research, education, and the open exchange of ideas between professions and across national or cultural borders.

They publish the *Journal of Small Business Management*, the *ICSB Bulletin,* and the proceedings of the annual meeting.

International Council for Small Business
c/o Center for Technology Development
105 Harris Hall
University of Missouri-Rolla
Rolla, MO 65401
Phone (314) 658-3896

8. The **National Association for the Self-Employed** has a membership of over 100,000 who have joined together to share access to benefits usually reserved for large corporations. Programs include health insurance, prescription savings, dental plans, representatives in Washington, toll-free business consulting, and travel discounts for both business and pleasure.

They publish *Small Business America*, a bimonthly newsletter. Membership is $48 a year. You can join by phone at 1-800-433-8004.

National Association for the Self-Employed
2316 Gravel Road
Fort Worth, TX 76118

9. The **National Coalition for Women's Enterprise, Inc.** acts as an advocate and information clearinghouse for women's self-employment issues. They also work on a

local level with committees to create women's self-employment programs.

National Coalition for Women's Enterprise, Inc.
30 Irving Place, 9th Floor
New York, NY 10003
Phone Marcia Cantarella, Executive Director, at (212) 505-2090

10. The **International Women's Networking Business Conference** (IWNBC) was founded to promote worldwide networking links among women in business and entrepreneurs from developed and non-industrialized nations for capital investment and joint ventures. Efforts by businesswomen to make a viable contribution to the economy of their respective countries is supported. IWNBC's trade missions are undertaken semi-annually to provide participants new contacts for import/export trading. The trade missions provide "hands-on" trade experience and expose to each country's regulatory requirements.
A newsletter is published twice yearly. Membership is $65 for individuals and $250 for corporations.

IWNBC
Farragut Park Bldg., Suite 204
1701 K St. N.W.
Washington, DC 20006
Phone Dolores Gregorio, President, at (202) 331-2142

11. The **American Business Women's Association** has 100,000 members and 2,100 chapters. The purpose is to bring together business women of diverse backgrounds to enhance personal and professional growth through leadership, education, networking support and national recognition.

American Business Women's Association
P O Box 8728
9100 Ward Parkway

Kansas City, MO 64114
Phone Carolyn B. Elman, Executive Director, at (816) 361-6621

12. The **Women's Economic Development Corp.** provides business development consulting, classes, and financing for Minnesota women starting or expanding a business. They publish *The Business of Small Business*, three workbooks for the woman entrepreneur, *The WEDCO Series Audio Tapes: Visualizing Success*. Their fees are on a sliding scale based on household income.

Women's Economic Development Corp.
1885 University Avenue West
Iris Park Place, Suite 315
St. Paul, MN 55104
Attn: Ms. Kathryn Keeley, President

13. The **American Association of Black Women Entrepreneurs** is a national network of minority women business owners. They offer training, publicity, and access to public officials.
They publish a newsletter and conference journals. Membership is $100 for business owners and $500 for organizations or large corporations.

American Association of Black Women Entrepreneurs
814 Thayer Avenue Suite 202A
Silver Spring, Maryland 20910
Phone Brenda Alford, President, at (301) 565-0527

14. **Women Construction Owners and Executives, USA** is a national association organized to promote business opportunities for women-owned businesses and the woman executive in the contruction industry. They offer national and regional newsletters, networking, business contacts, a resource center, a legislative access.
They publish national and regional newsletters.
Membership is $150 to $250 per year.

WCOE
P.O. Box 883034
San Francisco, CA 94188-3034
Phone Ms. Deborah Wilder, Executive Director, at (415) 467-2140.

15. The **National Enrepreneurship Education Consortium** promotes entrepreneurship education in high schools, two year colleges, and adult education. Membership provides resources to develop new curriculum, sponsor an annual forum, andshare materials and new programs in entrepreneurship education.
They have a number of publications.
Membership is $3000 per state and $500 for associates.

National Entrepreneurship Education Consortium
Center on Education and Training for Employment
Ohio State University
1900 Kenny Road
Columbus, Ohio 43210
Phone Dr. Catherine Ashmore, toll free, (800) 848-4815 or (614) 292-4353.

16. **The National Association of Home Based Businesses** provides marketing services such as catalogs, joint advertising mailers, business expos and a national distribution network and mail order service. They publish a newspaper.
Membership is $125 (initial fee) for full members, $65 for affiliate members, and $350 for professional consultants.

National Association of Home Based Businesses
P. O. Box 30220
Baltimore, MD 21270
Phone Cynthia Brower (301) 363-3698

Appendix 2

USEFUL BOOKS AND PAMPHLETS

1. *Free Money For Small Businesses and Entrepreneurs* by Laurie Blum lists over 300 sources including foundations, state and local government agencies and private funds. She also gives examples of successful grant proposals.
1988, ISBN 0 471-85802-1, John Wiley & Sons, $12.95.

2. *The Partnership Book, How to Write Your Own Small Business Partnership Agreement* by Attorneys Denis Clifford and Ralph Warner shows how to draft your own agreement. This book supplies a number of sample agreements which you can use as is. Buy-out clauses, unequal sharing of assets, financial liabilities, and limited partnerships are discussed in detail.
1987, ISBN 0-87337-041-4, Nolo Press, $18.95.
AVAILABLE FROM PUMA'S BUSINESS BOOKSHELF – SEE INSIDE BACK COVER

3. *Exporter's Guide to Federal Resources for Small Business* by American Telephone and Telegraph and the U.S. Small Business Administration describes all programs pertaining to exporting. It contains hundreds of names, phone numbers and addresses for specific questions.

$3.50. Request publication stock no. 045-000-00248-9 from one of the Government Printing Office Bookstores in Appendix III. They take telephone orders with credit cards.

4. *Small-Time Operator: How To Start Your Own Business, Keep Your Books, Pay Your Taxes, and Stay Out of Trouble* by Bernard Kamoroff. This is one of our favorites and is a bestseller, having about 250,000 in print. If keeping books and accounting is confusing, you need this book.

1988, ISBN 0-917510-06-2, Bell Springs Press, $11.95.

AVAILABLE FROM PUMA'S BUSINESS BOOK-SHELF – SEE INSIDE BACK COVER

5. *Starting and Managing a Business from Your Home* by the Small Business Administration. Covers assessing skills, evaluating your product and market, setting a price, how to structure and finance, zoning, insurance, and more.

1986 SBA. Send $1.75 to Consumer Information Center-G, P O Box 100, Pueblo, CO 81002. Ask for booklet 155T.

6. *The Business Planning Guide: Creating a Plan for Success in Your Business* by Andy Bangs. Another bestseller, this book is used by hundreds of banks and colleges to help owners put together a business plan.

1988, ISBN 0-936894-10-5, Upstart Publishing, $16.95.

AVAILABLE FROM PUMA'S BUSINESS BOOK-SHELF – SEE INSIDE BACK COVER

7. *Getting Yours* by Matthew Lesko contains descriptions of federal programs for all interests, e.g., the arts, education, health, veterans, urban renewal.

1987, ISBN 0-14046-652-5, Viking, $7.95.

8. *Marketing Without Advertising* by Michael Phillips and Salli Rosberry explains why most advertising is a waste of money and what constitutes effective promotion. Practical ways to increase sales with little investment are described.

1987, ISBN 0-87337-019-8, Nolo Press, $13.95.

AVAILABLE FROM PUMA'S BUSINESS BOOK-SHELF – SEE INSIDE BACK COVER

9. *Franchise Opportunities Handbook* by the Department of Commerce. The handbook lists all the franchises

available in the U.S.A., approximate start-up costs, and where to get more information.

1988, U.S. Government Printing Office, $16.00.

Phone the closest Government Printing Office Bookstore listed in Appendix III. They take credit cards.

10. *Advertising In the Yellow Pages, How to Boost Profits and Avoid Pitfalls* by W. F. Wagner is essential if the type of business you have is dependent on Yellow Pages advertising. Be sure to read it BEFORE meeting with a representative of the Yellow Pages.

1986, ISBN 0-940969-00-9, Harvest Press, $12.95.

AVAILABLE FROM PUMA'S BUSINESS BOOK-SHELF – SEE INSIDE BACK COVER

Appendix 3

HANDY TELEPHONE NUMBERS

1. Small Business Answer Desk. Small Business Administration staff is assigned to answer questions or refer you to appropriate government agencies. Monday through Friday, 7 am to 5 pm. Toll free (800) 368-5855. In Washington, DC, call 653-7561.

2. Business Assistance, Department of Commerce. Assistance in getting information concerning business from any government agency. (202) 377-3176.

3. Loans for Youngsters. Youngsters age 10 to 21 can get money for business ventures from the Department of Agriculture. Ask for **Youth Project Loan** pamphlet at (202) 382-1632.

4. To get the name of an expert on any subject you can think of, call the Library of Congress Referral Service (202) 287-5670.

5. Export-Import Bank, Small Business Advice. Call toll free (800) 424-5201. In Washington, DC, call 566-8860.
6. Agriculture Economic Data. For a recording of the latest agriculture economic news, call (202) 488-8358.

7. Product Safety Information. Call toll-free (800) 638-2772. In Maryland, call (301) 452-6626.

8. Federal Home Loan Bank, Information. Call toll free (800) 424-5405. In Washington, DC, call (202) 377-6988.

9. Solar Information, Department of Housing and Urban Development. Call toll free (800) 523-2929. In Pennsylvania call (800) 462-4983. In Alaska and Hawaii, call (800) 523-4700.

10. Overseas Private Investment Corporation. Call toll free (800) 424-6742. In Washington D.C., call (202) 653-2800. In Alaska and Hawaii call (800) 424-9704.

11. Loans, Small Business Administration. Call toll free (800) 368-5855. In Washington, DC, call 653-7561.

12. Patents. For information on patents including qualified professionals to assist you, call (703) 557-5168.

13. Department of Transportation, Information and Referrals on Technical Assistance and Research. Toll free discontinued. Call DOT information (202) 366-4000.

14. Recorded Messages:
      Economic news (202) 393-4100
      Agriculture news (202) 488-1110
      Job Information Center (202) 737-9616
      The President's Daily Schedule (202) 456-2343
      Announcing News (800) 424-9090

15. Business Development in rural areas. For brochure on ATTRA (Appropriate Technology Transfer for Rural Areas) call toll free (800) 346-9140.

16. Publications, Small Business Administration. Call toll free (800) 368-5855. In Washington, DC, call (202) 653-6365.

17. To Call Your Congressman. (202) 224-3121. The switchboard will connect you with any Congressman's office.

18. To Find Government Experts, call the General Services Administration. They will find you a government expert on almost any subject. Call (202) 755-8660.

19. Reference Services for Business. Call the Department of Commerce Library at (202) 377-5511.

20. To Enter Government Oil and Gas Lottery, call the Bureau of Land Management for an application. (202) 343-5717.

21. Student Financial Aid. Call the Department of Education toll free at (800) 241-4710. In Georgia call (800) 282-1050.

22. Government Jobs. Call the Federal Job Information Center at (202) 737-9616.

23. Abandoned Mine Reclamation. Call the Department of Interior at (202) 343-7937.

24. Social Security. To find out how much Social Security benefits you will receive, request form SSA-7004. Call toll free (800) 937-2000. Grumpy clerk will answer.

SMALL BUSINESS TOLL-FREE NUMBERS

Agriculture Fraud Hotline	800/424-9121
Commerce Department Fraud Hotline	800/424-5197
Consumer Product Safety Commission	800/638-2772
Defense Fraud Hotline	800/424-9098
Deloitte, Haskins & Sells, CPA	800/843-2727
EPA Hazardous Waste Hotline	800/424-9346
EPA Small Business Hotline	800/368-5888

EPA Radon Hotline	800/334-8571
EPA Asbestos Hotline	800/334-8571
Energy Inquiry and Referral (Energy Dept.)	
	800/523-2929
Export-Import Bank	800/424-5201
Fair Housing and Equal Opportunity (HUD)	
	800/424-8590
Federal Crime Insurance	800/638-8780
Federal Deposit Insurance Corporation	
	800/424-5488
Federal Election Commission	800/424-9530
Federal Home Loan Bank Board	800/424-5405
Flood Insurance	800/638-6620
General Accounting Office Fraud Hotline	
	800/424-5454
Health Info Clearinghouse (HHS)	800/336-4797
Highway Traffic Safety Administration	800/424-9393
Housing Discrimination Hotline (HUD)	
	800/424-8590
Interior Dept. Fraud Hotline	800/424-5081
Internal Revenue Service	800/424-1040
Labor Fraud Hotline	800/424-5409
National Technical Information Service	
	800/336-4700
Overseas Private Investment Corporation	
	800/424-6742
Small Business Answer Desk	800/368-5855
SBA-PASS users and large corporations	
	800/231-PASS
SBA/IRS Disaster Collection (in Alabama only)	
	800/654-2071
Talking Books Program (Library of Congress)	
	800/424-9100
Veterans Administration Fraud Hotline	
	800/368-5899
Women's Economic Development Corps NYC, NY	

	800/222-2933
Young, Arthur, CPA (SBIR)	800/3HI-TECH

SBA CENTRAL OFFICE PROGRAM NUMBERS

Office Number

Office	Number
Administrator	202/653-6605
Advisory Councils	653-6892
Business Development	653-6881
Congressional Relations	653-7581
Disaster Assistance	653-6879
Economic Development	503/653-6416
Employee Locator	653-6600
Equal Opportunity	653-6050
Financial Assistance	653-6574
Financial Institutions	653-2585
Freedom of Information	653-6460
General Counsel	653-6642
Hearing and Appeals	653-6805
Inspector General	653-6597
International Trade	653-7794
Law Library	653-6556
SBA Library	653-6914
Loan Processing	653-6470
Minority	653-6407
PASS	653-6442
Pollution Control Loans	653-2548
Private Sector Initiatives (incubators)	653-7880
Procurement (8a)	653-6813
Procurement	653-6938
Public Communications	653-6832
Reference Library	653-6913
SCORE/ACE	653-6279
Secondary Market Activity	212/264-5877
Size Standards	653-6373
Small Business Development Center	653-6768
Small Business Innovation Research-SBIR	653-6458

Small Business Institute-SBI	653-6628
Surety Bond (Ballston)	703/235-2900
Veterans Affairs	653-8220
Women's Business	653-8000

GENERAL SERVICES ADMINISTRATION

SMALL BUSINESS SERVICE CENTERS

Region	Address	Telephone
National Capital	7th & D Streets. NW Washington, DC 20407	202-472-1804
I	John W. McCormack Federal Building Boston, MA 02222	617-565-8100
II	26 Federal Plaza New York, NY 10278	212-264-1234
III	9th & Market Streets Philadelphia, PA 19107	215-597-9613
IV	75 Spring St. SW Atlanta, GA 30303	404-331-5103
V	230 S. Dearborn St. Chicago, IL 60604	312-353-5383
VI	1500 E. Bannister Rd. Kansas City, MO 64131	816-926-7203
VII	819 Taylor St. Fort Worth, TX 76102	817-334-3284
VIII	Denver Federal Center	303-236-7407

                    Building 41
                    Denver, CO 80225

IX   525 Market St.   415-974-0523
                    San Francisco, CA 94105

                    300 N. Los Angeles   213-894-3210
                    Los Angeles, CA 90012

X   Room 2413   206-931-7957
                    13th & C St. SW
                    Auburn, WA 98001

GOVERNMENT PRINTING OFFICE BOOK STORES

Alabama
  Birmingham, 9220-B Parkway East   205-731-1056
California
  Los Angeles, ARCO Plaza, 505 S. Flower St.
                                      213-894-5841
  San Francisco, 450 Golden Gate Ave 415-556-0642
Colorado
  Denver, 1961 Stout St.   303-844-3964
  Pueblo, 720 N. Main Majestic Bldg. 303-554-3142
Florida
  Jacksonville, 400 W. Bay St.   904-791-3801
Georgia
  Atlanta, 275 Peachtree St. NE   404-331-6947
Illinois
  Chicago, 219 S. Dearborn St.   312-353-5133
Massachusetts
  Boston, John F. Kennedy Federal Bldg., Sudbury St.
                                      617-565-2488
Michigan
  Detroit, 477 Michigan Ave.   313-226-7816
Missouri
  Kansas City, 601 E. 12th St.   816-765-2256

Ohio

    Cleveland, 1240 E. 9th St.   216-522-4922

    Columbus, 200 N. High St.   614-469-6956

Pennsylvania

    Philadelphia, 100 N. 17th St.   215-597-0677

    Pittsburgh, 1000 Liberty Ave.   412-644-2721

Texas

    Dallas, 1100 Commerce St.   214-767-0076

    Houston, College Center, 9319 Gulf Freeway

                        713-229-3515

Washington

    Seattle, 915 Second Ave.   206-442-2091

Washington, D.C. area

    Main Bookstore, 710 N. Capitol St.   202-275-2091

    Commerce Department, Pennsylvania Ave., N.W.

                        202-377-3527

    Retail Sales Branch, 8660 Cherry Lane, Laurel, MD

                        301-953-7974

    1717 H. Street, N.W., Washington, D.C.

                        202-653-5075

Wisconsin

    Milwaukee, 519 E. Wisconsin Ave.   414-291-1304

Note: Publications may be ordered by phone and charged to a major credit card.

INDEX

⒯he Business Bookshelf

These books have been carefully selected as the best on these subjects. **Your satisfaction is guaranteed or your money back.**

To order, call toll-free 1-800-255-5730 ext. 110. In Colorado, call (303) 872-8924 ext. 110. Please have your Visa or Mastercard ready.

Small Time Operator:
How to Start Your Own Business, Keep Your Books, Pay Your Taxes, and Stay Out of Trouble

By Bernard Kamoroff, C.P.A. The most popular small business book in the U.S., it's used by over 250,000 businesses. Easy to read and use, Small Time Operator is particularly good for those without bookkeeping experience. Comes complete with a year's supply of ledgers and worksheets designed especially for small businesses, and contains invaluable information on permits, licenses, financing, loans, insurance, bank accounts, etc.

ISBN 0-917510-06-2 190 pages 8-1/2 x 11 paperbound $12.95

The Business Planning Guide
Creating a Plan for Success in Your Own Business

By Andy Bangs. *The Business Planning Guide* has been used by hundreds of banks, colleges, and accounting firms to guide business owners through the process of putting together a complete and effective business plan and financing proposal. The *Guide* comes complete with examples, forms and worksheets that make the planning process painless. With over 150,000 copies in print, the *Guide* has become a small business classic.

ISBN 0-936894-10-5 149 pages 8-1/2 x 11 paperbound $16.95

**Puma Publishing • 1670 Coral Drive, Suite H
Santa Maria, California 93454**

HOW TO GET AN UPDATE ON
THE INFORMATION IN *FREE HELP*

We try to make each printing as correct and up-to-date as possible, however, changes after we go to print are inevitable.

For a FREE update;
- If you discover an incorrect phone number, change of personnel, discontinued program, or a *new* program of interest to *Free Help* readers, tell us about it and we'll send you a *free* update.
Or;
- Tell us what in *Free Help* was most or least helpful, suggestions for improvements, or give us a compliment and we'll send you a *free* update.
Or;
- If you've had a good experience with a particular government program, tell us about it and we'll send you a *free* update. If your experience is used in a future edition, full credit will be given   *Plus you may have a free book of your choice from our business book shelf* (see pages 205 and 206).

Updates are also available by sending $1.00 and a self addressed stamped business size envelope.

Be sure to give us the print date off the copyright page so we can send the proper update.

Puma Publishing
Suite H, 1670 Coral Drive, Santa Maria, CA 93454

5504